D1121838

WODEHOUSE
NUGGETS

WODEHOUSE NUGGETS

Selected by

Richard Usborne

HUTCHINSON
London Melbourne Sydney Auckland Johannesburg

To Jack Collard

Hutchinson & Co. (Publishers) Ltd

An imprint of the Hutchinson Publishing Group

17–21 Conway Street, London W1P 6JD

Hutchinson Group (Australia) Pty Ltd
30–32 Cremorne Street, Richmond South, Victoria 3121
PO Box 151, Broadway, New South Wales 2007

Hutchinson Group (NZ) Ltd
32–34 View Road, PO Box 40-086, Glenfield, Auckland 10

Hutchinson Group (SA) (Pty) Ltd
PO Box 337, Bergvlei 2012, South Africa

This selection first published 1983
© The Estate of P. G. Wodehouse 1983
© Selections and introduction Richard Usborne 1983
Decorative line drawings by Martin Williams
© Hutchinson & Co. (Publishers) Ltd 1983

Set in VIP Baskerville by
D. P. Media Limited, Hitchin, Hertfordshire

Printed in Great Britain by The Anchor Press Ltd
and bound by Wm Brendon & Son Ltd,
both of Tiptree, Essex

British Library in Cataloguing in Publication Data

Wodehouse, P. G.
  Wodehouse nuggets.
  I. Title   II. Usborne, Richard
828′.91207   PR6045.053

ISBN 0 09 152480 6

CONTENTS

INTRODUCTION

The *Penguin Dictionary of Modern Quotations* gives sixty-nine from Wodehouse – nuggets, nifties, one-liners, goodies or, to be pompous, verbal felicities. Sixty-nine? That's fewer than one per book. Evelyn Waugh said that Wodehouse's books had 'three uniquely brilliant and entirely original similes to each page'. In similes alone this would bring the potential nuggets count up to . . . well, you must work it out, but it comes to a lot of thousands.

There are fewer than two thousand here, and, if you reread Wodehouse's ninety-odd books, I expect you could find hundreds that you'd prefer to the ones I have picked.

All the illustrations in this book come from the now-deceased *Strand Magazine*, which published more than 150 of Wodehouse's stories over a period of thirty years. The picture on pages 3 and 159 shows Lord Emsworth happily dreaming, with his favourite book, Whiffle's *On The Care of the Pig*, fallen to the floor. Lord Emsworth's own beloved, prizewinning Empress of Blandings is, of course, a Black Berkshire.

RICHARD USBORNE

AUNTS
— AND —
UNCLES

In this life it is not aunts that matter but the courage which one brings to them.
The Mating Season, 1949

The spectacle of an uncle, even if only an uncle by marriage, going down for the third time in a sea of dance champagne, can never be an agreeable one.
Joy in the Morning, 1947

Like so many aunts, she was gifted with a sort of second sight.
Uncle Fred in the Springtime, 1939

A strange, almost unearthly light comes into the eyes of wronged uncles when they see a chance of getting a bit of their own back from erring nephews.
Uncle Dynamite, 1948

A covey of mildewed females whom he had classified under the general heading of Aunts.
'Goodbye to All Cats', *Young Men in Spats*, 1936

In the evening of his life his uncle Frederick, Lord Ickenham, still retained, together with a juvenile waist-line, the bright enthusiasms and the fresh, unspoiled mental outlook of a slightly inebriated undergraduate.
Uncle Dynamite, 1948

'I had an aunt who pawned my father's false teeth in order to contribute to the mission for propagating the gospel among the unenlightened natives of West Africa. Grilled subsequently by the family she said she was laying up treasure in heaven. . . .'
The Girl in Blue, 1970

Aunt Dahlia can turn in a flash into a carbon copy of a Duchess of the old school reducing an underling to a spot of grease, and what is so remarkable is that she doesn't have to use a lorgnette; just does it all with the power of the human eye.

Much Obliged, Jeeves, 1971

The aunt made a hobby of collecting dry seaweed, which she pressed and pasted in an album. One sometimes thinks that aunts live entirely for pleasure.

'The Rough Stuff', *The Clicking of Cuthbert*, 1922

'I remember years ago, Bertie,' said Aunt Dahlia, 'when you nearly swallowed your rubber comforter and started turning purple. And I, ass that I was, took it out and saved your life. Let me tell you, it will go very hard with you if you ever swallow a rubber comforter again when only I am by to aid.'

Right Ho, Jeeves, 1934

The sort of house you take a look at and say to yourself, 'Somebody's aunt lives there'.

'Without the Option', *Carry On, Jeeves*, 1925

My uncle George discovered that alcohol was a food well in advance of modern medical thought.

'The Delayed Exit of Claude and Eustace', *The Inimitable Jeeves*, 1923

My Aunt Dahlia has a carrying voice. . . . If all other sources of income failed, she could make a good living calling the cattle home across the Sands of Dee.

'Jeeves and the Song of Songs', *Very Good, Jeeves*, 1930

You don't often find an aunt taking the rap when she has a nephew at her disposal to shove the thing on to. It is pretty universally agreed that that is what nephews are for.

Aunts Aren't Gentlemen, 1974

If Esmond Haddock goes with a bang at the concert, as I anticipate, it won't be long before those aunts of his will be climbing trees and pulling them up after them whenever he looks squiggle-eyed at them.

The Mating Season, 1949

Aunt Agatha's demeanour now was rather like that of one who, picking daisies on the railway, has just caught the down express in the small of the back.

'Aunt Agatha Takes the Count', *The Inimitable Jeeves*, 1923

Uncle Percy soared skywards with a wordless squeak, obviously startled out of a year's growth.

Joy in the Morning, 1947

It almost seemed as if another of my quick trips to America would be rendered necessary. About the only advantage of having an aunt like Aunt Agatha is that it makes one travel, thus broadening the mind and enabling one to see new faces.

Joy in the Morning, 1947

'Where's your pride, Bertie?' said Aunt Dahlia, 'Have you forgotten your illustrious ancestors? There was a Wooster at the time of the Crusades who would have won the Battle of Joppa singlehanded, if he hadn't fallen off his horse.'

Aunts Aren't Gentlemen, 1974

Aunt Dahlia guffawed more liberally than I had ever heard a woman guffaw. If there had been an aisle, she would have rolled in it. . . . She was giving the impression of a hyena which had just heard a good one from another hyena.

Much Obliged, Jeeves, 1971

Many a fellow who looks like the dominant male and has himself photographed smoking a pipe curls up like carbon paper when confronted by an aunt.

The Mating Season, 1949

It is bad to be trapped in a den of slavering aunts, lashing their tails and glaring at you out of their red eyes.

The Mating Season, 1949

On the occasions when I have met Ukridge's Aunt Julia, I have felt the curious illusion of having just committed some particularly unsavoury crime and – what is more – of having done it

with swollen hands, enlarged feet, and trousers bagging at the knee on a morning when I had omitted to shave.
'A Bit of Luck for Mabel', *Eggs, Beans and Crumpets*, 1940

The fact that he had heard Horace speak of his Uncle Alaric as a baldheaded old coot with a walrus moustache had enabled him to identify the newcomer without difficulty. Few coots could have had less hair than this man, and any walrus would have been proud to possess the moustache at which he was puffing.
Uncle Fred in the Springtime, 1939

Lord Ickenham moved forward with elastic step and folded the girl in a warm embrace. It seemed to Pongo, not for the first time, that his uncle went out of his way to kiss girls. On the present occasion, a fatherly nod would amply have met the case.
Uncle Fred in the Springtime, 1939

James's uncle had just about enough brain to make a jay-bird fly crooked.
'Out of School', *The Man Upstairs*, 1914

Ricky turned on the Duke of Dunstable. 'You are without exception the worst tick and bounder that ever got fatty degeneration of the heart through half a century of gorging food and swilling wine wrenched from the lips of a starving proletariat. You make me sick. You poison the air. Good-bye, Uncle Alaric,' said Ricky, drawing himself away rather ostentatiously. 'I think we had better terminate this interview, or I may become brusque.'
Uncle Fred in the Springtime, 1939

The girl laughed – the gay, wholehearted laugh of youth. Pongo remembered that he had laughed like that in the days before he had begun to see so much of his Uncle Fred.
Uncle Fred in the Springtime, 1939

The uncle may have struck it rich in sheep or something out in Australia. Most uncles come from Australia.
A Prefect's Uncle, 1903

There came from without the hoof-beats of a galloping relative, and Aunt Dahlia whizzed in.
The Code of the Woosters, 1938

A fellow like himself – steady, upright, impervious to avuncular wheedlings and true blue from soup to nuts.
Uncle Dynamite, 1948

'Whether or not Aunt Julia said "My hero!" I am not certain,' said Ukridge. 'It was what she ought to have said, but she is a woman who is apt to miss her cues at times. However, she did clasp my hand in a fevered clutch, and with a brief word bidding her keep her tail up I went out.'
'Success Story', *Nothing Serious*, 1950

Pongo lit a reverent cigarette. He did not approve of his Uncle Fred, but he could not but admire his work.
Uncle Fred in the Springtime, 1939

Aunt Dahlia was staring at Jeeves like a bear about to receive a bun.
Jeeves and the Feudal Spirit, 1954

My Aunt Dahlia loves me dearly. I'm not saying her manner towards me doesn't verge at times on the brusque. In childhood days she would occasionally clump me on the side of the head, and since I have grown to riper years she has more than once begged me to tie a brick round my neck and go and drown myself in the pond in the kitchen garden. Nevertheless she loves her Bertram, and if she heard I was to be shot at sunrise, she would, as you say, be sore as a gumboil.
Jeeves in the Offing, 1960

My Aunt Agatha once went in for politics, but it only took a few meetings at which she got the bird from hecklers to convince her that the cagey thing to do was to stay at home and attend to her fancy needlework.
Stiff Upper Lip, Jeeves, 1963

I believe that Aunt Dahlia in her prime could lift fellow-members of the Quorn and Pytchley out of their saddles with a single yip, though separated from them by two ploughed fields and a spinney.
Jeeves in the Offing, 1960

Pongo quailed when he heard his uncle speak of the London air causing the sap to rise strongly in his veins. It seemed to suggest that his relative was planning to express and fulfil himself again, and when Frederick Altamont Cornwallis Twistleton, fifth Earl

of Ickenham, began to express and fulfil himself, strong men –
Pongo was one of them – quivered like tuning forks.
    Cocktail Time, 1958

He cowered before Aunt Dahlia like a wet sock.
    The Code of the Woosters, 1938

'Who has the star bedroom? Me? No! Uncle Aylmer. Who
collars the morning paper? Me? No! Uncle Aylmer. Who gets
the brown egg at breakfast? Me? No! Uncle Aylmer.'
    Uncle Dynamite, 1948

Her words did not appear to me to make sense. They seemed the
mere aimless vapouring of an aunt who has been sitting out in
the sun without a hat.
    Right Ho, Jeeves, 1934

On the occasions when Aunt is calling to Aunt like mastodons
bellowing across primeval swamps, and Uncle James's letter
about Cousin Mabel's peculiar behaviour is being shot round
the family circle ('Please read this carefully and send it on to
Jane'), the clan has a tendency to ignore me.
    'The Delayed Exit of Claude and Eustace', *The Inimitable
    Jeeves*, 1923

'Your Aunt Agatha made her husband knock off smoking the
other day, and he behaved like a cinnamon bear with its foot in a
trap.'
    Jeeves and the Feudal Spirit, 1954

The trouble about talking to a sister like a Dutch uncle is that
she is very apt to come right back at you and start talking to you
like a Dutch aunt.
    Pigs Have Wings, 1952

. . . a bleak, austere expression. She was looking more like an
aunt than anything human. In his boyhood he had observed
platoons of his aunts with their features frozen in a similar

rigidity. To name but one, his Aunt Charlotte on the occasion when he had been led into her presence, charged with having broken the curate's umbrella.
Barmy in Wonderland, 1952

Few women would have been in a vivacious mood, had Fate touched off beneath them a similar stick of trinitrotoluol. Aunt Dahlia's emotions must have been of much the same nature as those which she had no doubt frequently experienced in her hunting days when her steed, having bucked her from the saddle, had proceeded to roll on her.
Jeeves and the Feudal Spirit, 1954

Pongo had noticed on his uncle's face a lurking gleam such as one might discern in the eye of a small boy who has been left alone in the house and knows where the key of the jam cupboard is.
Uncle Dynamite, 1948

I have always had the suspicion that Aunt Dahlia, while invariably matey and bonhomous and seeming to take pleasure in my society, has a lower opinion of my intelligence than I quite like. Too often it is her practice to address me as 'fathead', and if I put forward any little thought or idea or fancy in her hearing it is apt to be greeted with an affectionate but jarring guffaw.
'The Love That Purifies', *Very Good, Jeeves*, 1930

A keen observer might have noticed a defensiveness in her manner. She looked like a girl preparing to cope with an aunt.
Summer Lightning, 1929

Her niece Millicent was to be united to a young man who, besides being penniless, had always afflicted her with a nervous complaint for which she could find no name, but which is known to scientists as the heeby-jeebies.
Summer Lightning, 1929

He was trying to conjure up a picture of a benevolent uncle patting him on the head with one hand while writing cheques with the other. . . .
Summer Lightning, 1929

Aunt Dahlia uttered a startled hunting cry. Uncle Tom, who probably imagined from the noise that this was civilisation crashing at last, helped things along by breaking a coffee cup.
Right Ho, Jeeves, 1934

'You know the pond at the end of the kitchen garden?' said Aunt Dahlia. 'Get a good, stout piece of rope or cord and look about till you find a nice, heavy stone. Or a fairly large brick would do. Then fasten the rope to the brick and tie it round your damned neck and jump into the pond and drown yourself. In a few days I will send and have you fished up and buried because I shall need to dance on your grave.'
Right Ho, Jeeves, 1934

Even at normal times Aunt Dahlia's map tended a little towards the crushed strawberry. But never had I seen it take on so pronounced a richness as now. She looked like a tomato struggling for self-expression.
Right Ho, Jeeves, 1934

For some moments there was nothing to be heard but the sloshing sound of an aunt restoring her tissues.
Right Ho, Jeeves, 1934

My Uncle Tom has a peculiarity I've noticed in other very oofy men. Nick him for the paltriest sum, and he lets out a squawk you can hear at Land's End. He has the stuff in gobs, but he hates giving it up.
Right Ho, Jeeves, 1934

'My Aunt Myrtle became the only woman in East Dulwich who could truthfully say she had bitten off her own toe. . . .'
The Girl in Blue, 1970

Aunt Dahlia uttered a cry like a wail of a master of hounds seeing a fox shot.
Right Ho, Jeeves, 1934

Any capable aunt can give Scotland Yard inspectors strokes and a bisque in the matter of interrogating a suspect, and I knew all attempts at concealment would be fruitless. Or is it bootless? I would have to check with Jeeves.
Much Obliged, Jeeves, 1971

Aunts as a class are like Napoleon. They expect their orders to be carried out without a hitch and don't listen to excuses.
Much Obliged, Jeeves, 1971

As I approached the door, I suddenly observed that there hung over it a striking portrait of Aunt Agatha, from the waist upwards. It caught my eye and halted me in my tracks as though I had run into a lamp-post. It was the work of one of those artists who reveal the soul of the sitter, and it had revealed so much of Aunt Agatha's soul that for all practical purposes it might have been that danger to traffic in person. Indeed, I came within an ace of saying 'Hullo!' at the same moment when I could have sworn it said 'Bertie!' in that compelling voice that had so often rung in my ears and caused me to curl up in a ball in the hope that a meek subservience would enable me to get off lightly.
Joy in the Morning, 1947

CHURCH
—AND—
CHURCHMEN

Like so many vicars, he had a poor opinion of curates.
  'Mulliner's Buck-U-Uppo', *Meet Mr Mulliner*, 1927

The task of composing a sermon which should practically make
sense and yet not be above the heads of his rustic flock was
always one that caused Augustine Mulliner to concentrate
tensely. Soon he was lost in his labour and oblivious to everything but the problem of how to find a word of one syllable that
meant Supralapsarianism.
  'Gala Night', *Mulliner Nights*, 1933

'Unhappily,' said the bishop, 'my wife has instructed me to give
the vacant vicarage to a cousin of hers. A fellow,' he added
bitterly, 'who bleats like a sheep and doesn't know an alb from a
reredos.'
  'The Bishop's Move', *Meet Mr Mulliner*, 1927

The cook burst into tears and said something about the Wrath
of the Lord and the Cities of the Plain – she being a bit on the
Biblical side.
  'Ukridge and the Home from Home', *Lord Emsworth and
  Others*, 1937

Here was this man, unable as a clerk in Holy Orders to use any
of the words which would have been at the disposal of a layman,
and yet by sheer force of character rising triumphantly over the
handicap. Without saying a thing that couldn't have been said
in the strictest drawing-room, the Rev. Aubrey Upjohn con-
trived to produce in Freddie the illusion that he had had a
falling out with the bucko mate of a tramp steamer.
  'Bramley is So Bracing', *Nothing Serious*, 1950

'You know Mr Brotherhood, the curate. That nice young man
with the pimples. He has gone and got measles.'
  Uncle Dynamite, 1948

The vicar's theme was the Church Organ, and it was in a vein of pessimism that he spoke of its prospects. The Church Organ, he told us frankly, was in a hell of a bad way. For years it had been going around with holes in its socks, doing the Brother-can-you-spare-a-dime stuff, and now it was about due to hand in its dinner pail. There had been a time when he had hoped that the pull-together spirit might have given it a shot in the arm, but the way it looked to him at the moment, things had gone too far and he was prepared to bet his shirt on the bally contrivance going down the drain and staying there.
The Mating Season, 1949

My nephew Augustine [said Mr Mulliner] was a curate and he was very young and extremely pale. As a boy he had completely outgrown his strength, and I rather think at his Theological College some of the wilder spirits must have bullied him. He was as meek and mild a young man as you could meet in a day's journey. He had flaxen hair, weak blue eyes and the general demeanour of a saintly but timid cod-fish.
'Mulliner's Buck-U-Uppo', *Meet Mr Mulliner*, 1927

The Rev. Stanley Brandon was a huge and sinewy man of violent temper, whose red face and glittering eyes might well have intimidated the toughest curate. The Rev. Stanley had been a heavy-weight boxer at Cambridge, and I gather from my nephew Augustine, his curate, that he seemed to be always on the point of introducing into debates on parish matters the methods that had made him so successful in the roped ring. I remember Augustine telling me that once, on the occasion when he had ventured to oppose the other's views in the matter of decorating the church for the Harvest Festival, he thought for a moment that the vicar was going to drop him with a right hook to the chin. It was some quite trivial point that had come up – a question as to whether the pumpkin would look better in the apse or the clerestory, if I remember rightly – but for several seconds it seemed that blood was about to be shed.
'Mulliner's Buck-U-Uppo', *Meet Mr Mulliner*, 1927

'Your first sermon was a success?'

'Well, they didn't rush the pulpit.'

'You are too modest, Bill Bailey, I'll bet you had them rolling in the aisles and carried out on stretchers.'

Service with a Smile, 1962

She gave a sort of despairing gesture, like a vicar's daughter who has discovered Erastianism in the village.

Laughing Gas, 1936

The Rev. 'Stinker' Pinker was dripping with high principles. . . .

The Code of the Woosters, 1938

'I've seen the light,' said the policeman, hitherto an atheist, 'and what I wanted to ask you, sir, was do I have to join the Infants' Bible Class or can I start singing in the choir right away?'

The Mating Season, 1949

Country butter and the easy life these curates lead had added a pound or two to an always impressive figure. To find the lean, finely trained Stinker of my nonage, I felt that one would have to catch him in Lent.

The Code of the Woosters, 1938

'Not only were we scooped in and shanghaied to church twice on Sunday, regardless of age or sex, but on the Monday morning at eight o'clock – eight, mark you – there were family prayers in the dining room.'

'Fate', *Young Men in Spats*, 1936

'Uncle Watkyn will be so grateful that he will start spouting vicarages like a geyser.'

The Code of the Woosters, 1938

They train curates to judge bonny babies. At the theological colleges. Start them off with ventriloquists' dummies, I shouldn't wonder.

Uncle Dynamite, 1948

'I won't believe you're married until I see the bishop and assistant clergy mopping their foreheads and saying, "Well, that's that. We really got the young blighter off at last." '

Aunts Aren't Gentlemen, 1974

He liked his curates substantial, and Bill proved to be definitely the large economy size, the sort of curate whom one could picture giving the local backslider the choice between seeing the light or getting plugged in the eye.

Service with a Smile, 1962

'She is very far from being one of the boys. You needn't let it get about, of course, but that girl, to my certain knowledge, plays the organ in the local church and may often be seen taking soup to the deserving villagers with many a gracious word.'

'Fate', *Young Men in Spats*, 1936

It was one of those aloof smiles that the Honorary Secretary of a Bible Class might have given the elderly aunt of a promising pupil.

'Fate', *Young Men in Spats*, 1936

'You can't let Harold get it in the neck. You were telling me this afternoon that he would be unfrocked. I won't have him unfrocked. Where is he going to get if they unfrock him? That sort of thing gives a curate a frightful black eye.'

The Code of the Woosters, 1938

His trust in Bodmin the hatter is like the unspotted faith of a young curate in his Bishop.

'The Amazing Hat Mystery', *Young Men in Spats*, 1936

She looked like a vicar's daughter who plays hockey and ticks off the villagers when they want to marry their deceased wives' sisters.

Laughing Gas, 1936

'I have got to take a few pints of soup to the deserving poor,' said Myrtle. 'I'd better set about it. Amazing the way these bimbos absorb soup. Like sponges.'

'Anselm Gets his Chance', *Eggs, Beans and Crumpets*, 1940

England was littered with the shrivelled remains of curates at whom the lady bishopess had looked through her lorgnette. He had seen them wilt like salted snails at the episcopal breakfast table.

'Mulliner's Buck-U-Uppo', *Meet Mr Mulliner*, 1927

'That's what today's Church needs, more curates capable of hauling off and letting fellows like Spode have it where it does most good.'
Stiff Upper Lip, Jeeves, 1963

'Why, of course. I've got it,' said his Uncle Fred to Pongo. 'Your name shall be Glossop. Sir Roderick Glossop, as I see it, was one of two brothers and, as so often happens, the younger brother did not equal the elder's success in life. He became a curate, dreaming away the years in a country parish, and when he died, leaving only a copy of *Hymns Ancient and Modern*, and a son called Basil, Sir Roderick found himself stuck with the latter. So with the idea of saving something out of the wreck he made him his secretary. That's what I call a nice well-rounded story.'
Uncle Fred in the Springtime, 1939

A curate pal of mine in Limehouse had sprained his ankle while trying to teach the choir-boys to dance the carioca.
Service with a Smile, 1962

The Rev. 'Stinker' Pinker looked like a clerical beetroot.
The Code of the Woosters, 1938

She didn't like him being an atheist, and he wouldn't stop being an atheist, and finally he said something about Jonah and the Whale which it was impossible for her to overlook. This morning she returned the ring, his letters and a china ornament with 'A Present from Blackpool' on it which he had bought her last summer while visiting relatives in the north.
The Mating Season, 1949

The Bishop of Stortford was talking to the local Master of Hounds about the difficulty he had in keeping his vicars off the incense.
'Unpleasantness at Bludleigh Court', *Mr Mulliner Speaking*, 1929

'Any moment now, he may get a vicarage, and then watch his smoke. He'll be a Bishop some day.'

'A fat lot of bishing he's going to do, if he's caught sneaking helmets from members of his flock.'

The Code of the Woosters, 1938

Had Stinker encountered Spode on the football field, he would have had no hesitation in springing at his neck and twisting it into a lover's knot. The trouble was that he was a curate, and the brass hats of the Church look askance at curates who swat the parishioners. Swat your flock, and you're sunk. So now he shrank from intervening and when he did intervene, it was merely with the soft word that's supposed to turn away wrath.

'I say, you know, what?' he said.

Stiff Upper Lip, Jeeves, 1963

The Rev. Rupert Bingham seemed subdued and gloomy, as if he had discovered schism among his flock.

'Company for Gertrude', *Blandings Castle and Elsewhere*, 1935

On her face was the look of a mother whose daughter has seen the light and will shortly be marrying a deserving young clergyman with a bachelor uncle high up in the shipping business.

'The Go-Getter', *Blandings Castle and Elsewhere*, 1935

'Lay off the lotion,' Linda had said to him, or words to that effect, and he had said that he would. Even if the Archbishop of Canterbury were to come and beg him to join him in a few for the tonsils, no business would result.

Frozen Assets, 1964

With a quick, impulsive movement, like that of a man trying to rid himself of a dead fish, the Rev. 'Stinker' thrust the policeman's helmet at Stiffy, who received it with a soft, tender squeal of ecstasy.

The Code of the Woosters, 1938

A lady of the manor, with an important fête coming along and the curate in bed with measles, is in the distressing position of an impresario whose star fails him a couple of days before the big production or a general whose crack regiment gets lumbago on the eve of battle.
  Uncle Dynamite, 1948

From the vicar's own lips he had had it officially that the Mothers' Outing expedition should drive to the neighbouring village of Bottsford Mortimer, where there were the ruins of an old abbey, replete with interest; lunch among these ruins; visit the local museum (founded and presented to the village by the late Sir Wandesbury Pott, JP); and, after filling in with a bit of knitting, return home. And now the whole trend of the party appeared to be towards the Amusement Park on the Bridmouth pier.
  'Tried in the Furnace', *Young Men in Spats*, 1936

'Golly! When you admonish a congregation, it stays admonished!'
  'Anselm Gets his Chance', *Eggs, Beans and Crumpets*, 1940

LITERATURE
— AND —
ART

'The moment my fingers clutch a pen,' said Leila Yorke, 'a great change comes over me. I descend to the depths of goo which you with your pure mind wouldn't believe possible. I write about stalwart men, strong but oh so gentle, and girls with wide grey eyes and hair the colour of ripe wheat, who are always having misunderstandings and going to Africa. The men, that is. The girls stay at home and marry the wrong bimbos. But there's a happy ending. The bimbos break their necks in the hunting field and the men come back in the last chapter and they and the girls get together in the twilight, and all around is the scent of English flowers and birds singing their evensong in the shrubbery. Makes me shudder to think of it.'

Ice in the Bedroom, 1961

On paper, Blair Eggleston was bold, cold, and ruthless. Like so many of our younger novelists, his whole tone was that of a disillusioned, sardonic philanderer who had drunk the wine-cup of illicit love to its dregs but was always ready to fill up again and have another. There were passages in some of his books, notably *Worm i' the Root* and *Offal*, which simply made you shiver, so stark was their cynicism, so brutal the force with which they tore away the veils and revealed Woman as she is.

Deprived of his fountain-pen, however, Blair was rather timid with women. He had never actually found himself alone in an incense-scented studio with a scantily-clad princess reclining on a tiger skin, but in such a situation he would most certainly have taken a chair as near to the door as possible and talked about the weather.

Hot Water, 1932

The Sheridan Apartment House stands in the heart of New York's Bohemian and artistic quarter. If you threw a brick from any of its windows, you would be certain to brain some rising interior decorator, some Vorticist sculptor or a writer of revolutionary *vers libre*.

The Small Bachelor, 1927

Imagine how some unfortunate Master Criminal would feel, on coming down to do a murder at the Old Grange, if he found that not only was Sherlock Holmes putting in the week-end there, but Hercule Poirot as well.

The Code of the Woosters, 1938

If you were a millionaire, would you rather be stabbed in the back with a paperknife or found dead without a mark on you, staring with blank eyes at some appalling sight?

'Best Seller', *Mulliner Nights*, 1933

Ambrose isn't a frightfully hot writer. I don't suppose he makes enough out of a novel to keep a midget in doughnuts for a week. Not a really healthy midget.

The Luck of the Bodkins, 1935

She often asked him if he thought it quite nice to harp on sudden death and blackmailers with squints. Surely, she said, there were enough squinting blackmailers in the world without writing about them.

'Honeysuckle Cottage', *Meet Mr Mulliner*, 1927

The unpleasant, acrid smell of burnt poetry.

'The Fiery Wooing of Mordred', *Young Men in Spats*, 1936

Ambrose was a writer, but large and muscular, with keen eyes, a jutting chin, a high colour and hands like hams, and was apt, when on holiday, to dash off and go climbing the Pyrenees – and what's more, to sing while he did it.

The Luck of the Bodkins, 1935

He had never acted in his life and couldn't play the pin in *Pinafore*.

The Luck of the Bodkins, 1935

Dark hair fell in a sweep over his forehead. He looked like a man who would write *vers libre*, as indeed he did.

The Girl on the Boat, 1922

Writers through the ages have made a good many derogatory remarks about money and one gets the impression that it is a thing best steered clear of, but every now and then one finds people who like the stuff and one of these was Jane. It seemed to her to fill a long-felt want.

The Girl in Blue, 1970

In his office on the premises of Popgood and Grooly, publishers of the Book Beautiful, Madison Avenue, New York, Cyril Grooly, the firm's junior partner, was practising putts into a tooth glass and doing rather badly even for one with a twenty-four handicap, when Patricia Binstead, Mr Popgood's secretary, entered, and dropping his putter he folded her in a close embrace. This was not because all American publishers are warm-hearted impulsive men and she a very attractive girl, but because they had recently become betrothed. On his return from his summer vacation at Paradise Valley, due to begin this afternoon, they would step along to some convenient church and become man – if you can call someone with a twenty-four handicap a man – and wife.

'Sleepy Time', *Plum Pie*, 1966

He looked like a statue of Right Triumphing Over Wrong. You couldn't place it exactly because it was so long since you had read the book, but he reminded you of something out of *Pilgrim's Progress*.

'The Go-Getter', *Blandings Castle and Elsewhere*, 1935

Like all young artists nowadays, he had always held before him as the goal of his ambition the invention of some new comic animal for the motion pictures. What he burned to do, as Velazquez would have burned to do if he had lived today, was to think of another Mickey Mouse and then give up work and just sit back and watch the money roll in.

'Buried Treasure', *Lord Emsworth and Others*, 1937

I always bar the sort of story where Chapter Ten ends with the hero trapped in the underground den and Chapter Eleven starts with him being the life and soul of the gay party at the Spanish Embassy.

Thank You, Jeeves, 1934

The literary agent was a grim, hard-bitten person, to whom, when he called at their offices to arrange terms, editors kept their faces turned so that they might at least retain their back collar studs.

'Honeysuckle Cottage', *Meet Mr Mulliner*, 1927

Blair Eggleston was a man who wore side-whiskers and if the truth were known, was probably a secret beret-wearer as well.

Hot Water, 1932

The Dean's opinion of artists was low. He wrote to his nephew emphasising the grievous pain it gave him to think that one of his flesh and blood should deliberately be embarking on a career which must inevitably lead sooner or later to the painting of Russian princesses lying on divans in the semi-nude with their arms round tame jaguars. He urged Lancelot to return and become a curate while there was yet time.

'The Story of Webster', *Mulliner Nights*, 1933

Unlike most publishers, who tend to become lean and haggard through mixing with authors, he bulged opulently in all directions and with his round face, round eyes and round spectacles looked like an owl which has been doing itself too well on the field-mice.

French Leave, 1956

Of all the myriad individuals that went to make up the kaleidoscopic life of New York, Mrs Waddington disliked artists most. They never had any money. They were dissolute and feckless. They attended dances at Webster Hall in strange costumes and frequently played the ukelele.

The Small Bachelor, 1927

'Yes, sir, he's pining for the great wide open spaces of the West. He says the East is effete and he wants to be out there among the silent canyons where men are men. If you want to know what I think, somebody's been feeding him Zane Grey.'

The Small Bachelor, 1927

McCay was of a romantic and sentimental nature . . . the sort of man who keeps old ball programmes and bundles of letters tied round with lilac ribbon. . . . McCay knew Ella Wheeler Wilcox by heart, and could take Browning without anaesthetics.

'Archibald's Benefit', *The Man Upstairs*, 1914

It has been well said that an author who expects results from a first novel is in a position similar to that of a man who drops a rose petal down the Grand Canyon of Arizona and listens for the echo.

Cocktail Time, 1958

I shouldn't wonder if right from the start Mrs Bingo hasn't had a sort of sneaking regret that Bingo isn't one of those strong, curt, Empire-building kind of Englishmen she puts in her books, with sad, unfathomable eyes, lean, sensitive hands, and riding boots.

'Jeeves and the Old School Chum', *Very Good, Jeeves*, 1930

Corky was near the door, looking at the picture – a painting of a baby – with one hand up in a defensive sort of way, as if he thought it might swing on him.

'The Artistic Career of Corky', *Carry On, Jeeves*; 1925

'One of those ghastly literary lunches. I don't know why I go to them. It isn't as if I were like Jimmy Fothergill, fighting for a knighthood and not wanting to miss a trick. This one was to honour Emma Lucille Agee who wrote that dirty novel that's been selling in millions in America. . . . About fifteen of the dullest speeches I ever heard. The Agee woman told us for three quarters of an hour how she came to write her beastly book, when a simple apology was all that was required. . . .'

The Girl in Blue, 1970

I knew Chekhov's *Seagull*. My Aunt Agatha had once made me take her son Thos to a performance of it at the Old Vic, and what with the strain of trying to follow the cockeyed goings-on of characters called Zarietchnaya and Medvienko and having to be constantly on the alert to prevent Thos making a sneak for the great open spaces, my suffering had been intense.

Jeeves in the Offing, 1960

The rich contralto of a female novelist calling to its young had broken the stillness of the summer afternoon.

'Mr Potter Takes a Rest Cure', *Blandings Castle and Elsewhere*, 1935

'I may as well tell you that if you are going about the place thinking things pretty, you will never make a modern poet. Be poignant, man, be poignant!'

The Small Bachelor, 1927

For an instant Wilfred Allsop's face lit up, as that of the poet Shelley whom he so closely resembled must have done when he suddenly realised that 'blithe spirit' rhymes with 'near it', not that it does, and another ode as good as off the assembly line.
Galahad at Blandings, 1964

A man who wore a tie that went twice round the neck was sure, sooner or later, to inflict some hideous insult on helpless womanhood. Add tortoiseshell-rimmed glasses, and you had what practically amounted to a fiend in human shape.
'Best Seller', *Mulliner Nights*, 1933

Sam Bagsott wrote short, bright articles on fly fishing, healthy living, muscle development, great lovers through the ages, and the modern girl. He wrote light verse, reviews of novels, interviews with celebrities, chatty Guides to the Brontë country and the Land of Dickens, stories for half-witted adults, stories for retarded boys and stories for children with water on the brain.
Galahad at Blandings, 1964

The first sight of Boko reveals to the beholder an object with a face like an intellectual parrot. Furthermore, as is the case with so many of the younger literati, he dresses like a tramp cyclist . . . conveying a sort of general suggestion of having been left out in the rain overnight in an ash can.
Joy in the Morning, 1947

Private Investigator Adair's private investigations had apparently taken him elsewhere for the moment, to a consultation at Scotland Yard perhaps, or possibly to Joe the Lascar's opium den in Limehouse in connection with the affair of the Maharajah's Ruby.
Money in the Bank, 1946

I felt that if the thing was to be smacked into, 'twere well 'twere smacked into quickly, as Shakespeare says.
Joy in the Morning, 1947

He wrote stories about mysterious Chinamen and girls with hair the colour of ripe wheat and the corpses of baronets in panelled libraries.
Money in the Bank, 1946

'What a curse these social distractions are. They ought to be abolished. I remember saying that to Karl Marx once, and he thought there might be an idea for a book in it.'
Quick Service, 1940

The second mate of a tramp steamer or one of Miss Ethel M. Dell's more virile heroes might have attempted truculence with Mr Slingsby and got away with it, but Bill knew that he was not the man to do it.
Bill the Conqueror, 1924

'I had a private income – the young artist's best friend.'
Quick Service, 1940

Poets, as a class, are business men. Shakespeare describes the poet's eye as rolling in a fine frenzy from heaven to earth, from earth to heaven, and giving to airy nothing a local habitation and a name, but in practice you will find that one corner of that eye is generally glued on the royalty returns.
Uncle Fred in the Springtime, 1939

'I didn't know poets broke people's necks.'
'Ricky does. He once took on three simultaneous costermongers in Covent Garden and cleaned them up in five minutes. He had gone there to get inspiration for a pastoral, and they started chi-iking him, and he sailed in and knocked them base over apex into a pile of Brussels sprouts.'
'How different from the home life of the late Lord Tennyson.'
Uncle Fred in the Springtime, 1939

After marrying Anastatia Bates, he wrote mystery thrillers, and so skilful was his technique that he was soon able to push out his couple of thousand words of wholesome blood-stained fiction each morning before breakfast, leaving the rest of the day for the normal fifty-four holes of golf.
'Rodney Has a Relapse', *Nothing Serious*, 1950

If there is one thing that wakes the fiend which sleeps in all writers, it is getting stuck in the big chapter of a sunny and optimistic novel.
Bill the Conqueror, 1924

When a girl has been mixing for two years with the sort of blots who made up the personnel of our Parisian circle and somebody comes along who hasn't a beard and dresses well and looks as if he took a bath every morning instead of only at Christmas and on his birthday, something she may easily mistake for love awakes in her heart.

Frozen Assets, 1964

'You are probably not familiar with the inner workings of a paper like Society Spice, Sir Gregory, but I may tell you that it is foreign to the editorial policy ever to meet visitors who call with horsewhips.'

Summer Lightning, 1929

If Pippa had happened to pass at that moment, singing of God being in his Heaven and all right with the world, he would have shaken her by the hand and told her he knew just how she felt.

Uncle Dynamite, 1948

She wrote novels: and that instinct of self-preservation which lurks in every publisher had suggested to him that behind her invitation lay a sinister desire to read those to him one by one.

'Mr Potter Takes a Rest Cure', *Blandings Castle and Elsewhere*, 1935

Mr Potter, being, as are all publishers, more like a shrinking violet than anything else in the world, nearly swooned. His scalp tingled: his jaw fell: and his toes began to open and shut like poppet valves.

'Mr Potter Takes a Rest Cure', *Blandings Castle and Elsewhere*, 1935

His manner had nothing in it of the jolly innkeeper of old-fashioned comic opera. He looked more like Macbeth seeing a couple of Banquos.

Frozen Assets, 1964

'You mean he's a private eye? Now there's a thing I'd have liked to be. The fifth of bourbon in the desk drawer, the automatic in the holster and the lightly clad secretary on the lap. Yes, I've often wished I were a shamus.'

Frozen Assets, 1964

'I shall be editor of the *Thursday Review*, and that's a job I can hardly fail to hold down. I'm not likely to fire myself. If at first I make a mistake or two, I shall be very lenient and understanding.'

Jeeves in the Offing, 1960

To Lady Blake Somerset, who had been brought up on *Trilby*, no girl living in Paris could possibly have the smallest claim to respectability.

Frozen Assets, 1964

I admit that Madeline Bassett is pretty. Any red-blooded Sultan or Pasha, if offered the opportunity of adding her to the personnel of his harem, would jump to it without hesitation, but he would regret his impulsiveness before the end of the first week. She's one of those soppy girls, riddled from head to foot with whimsy. She holds the view that the stars are God's daisy chain, that rabbits are gnomes in attendance on the Fairy Queen, and that every time a fairy blows its wee nose a baby is born, which, as we know, is not the case.

Stiff Upper Lip, Jeeves, 1963

Freddie, when making his purchase at Clarkson's, had evidently preferred quantity to quality. The salesman, no doubt, had recommended something in neat Vandykes as worn by the better class of ambassadors, but Freddie was a hunted stag, and when hunted stags buy beards, they want something big and bushy as worn by Victorian novelists. Freddie could have stepped into the Garrick Club of the Sixties, and Wilkie Collins and the rest of the boys would have welcomed him as a brother, supposing him to be Walt Whitman.

'The Fat of the Land', *A Few Quick Ones*, 1959

Mr Howard Saxby, literary agent, was knitting a sock. He knitted a good deal, he would tell you if you asked him, to keep himself from smoking, adding that he also smoked a good deal to keep himself from knitting.

Cocktail Time, 1958

The question of how authors come to write their books is generally one not easily answered. Milton, for instance, asked how he got the idea for *Paradise Lost*, would probably have replied with a vague 'Oh, I don't know, you know. These things sort of pop into your head, don't you know,' leaving the researcher very much where he was before.

Cocktail Time, 1958

It so often pans out that way when you begin a story. You whizz off the mark all pep and ginger, like a mettlesome charger going into its routine, and the next thing you know, the customers are up on their hind legs, yelling for footnotes.

The Mating Season, 1949

I don't know if you ever came across a play of Shakespeare's called *Macbeth*? If you did, you may remember this bird Macbeth bumps off another bird named Banquo and gives a big dinner to celebrate, and picture his embarrassment when about the first of the gay throng to turn up is Banquo's ghost, all merry and bright, covered in blood. It gave him a pretty nasty start, Shakespeare does not attempt to conceal. But it was nothing to the start Bingo got on observing Nanny Byles in his midst. He felt as if he had been lolling in the electric chair at Sing Sing and some practical joker had suddenly turned on the juice.

'The Shadow Passes', *Nothing Serious*, 1950

Rodney Spelvin was in for another attack of poetry. . . . He had once been a poet, and a very virulent one, too; the sort of man who would produce a slim volume of verse bound in squashy mauve leather at the drop of a hat, mostly on the subject of sunsets and pixies.

'Rodney Has a Relapse', *Nothing Serious*, 1950

. . . that inevitability that was such a feature of the best Greek tragedy. Aeschylus once said to Euripides 'You can't beat inevitability,' and Euripides said he had often thought so, too.

Uncle Dynamite, 1948

Bingo sat down and wrote a story about a little girl called Gwendoline and her cat Tibby. The idea being, of course, to publish it in *Wee Tots* and clean up.

It was no easy task. Until he started on it he had no notion what blood, sweat and tears are demanded from the poor sap who takes a pop at the life literary, and a new admiration for Mrs Bingo awoke in him. Mrs Bingo, he knew, did her three thousand words a day without ricking a muscle, and to complete this Tibby number, though it ran only to about fifteen hundred, took him over a week, during which period he on several occasions as near as a toucher went off his onion.

'The Word in Season', *A Few Quick Ones*, 1959

George Gissing's books . . . as grey as a stevedore's vest.

Ice in the Bedroom, 1961

What the song needed was Tetrazzini, or someone who would just pick that note off the roof and hold it till the janitor came round to lock up the building for the night.

'Mother's Knee', *Indiscretions of Archie*, 1921

Freddie experienced the sort of abysmal soul-sadness which afflicts one of Tolstoi's Russian peasants when, after putting in a heavy day's work strangling his father, beating his wife, and dropping the baby into the city reservoir, he turns to the cupboard, only to find the vodka bottle empty.

Jill the Reckless, 1921

He had a mild fondness for letters, which took the form of meaning to read right through the hundred best books one day, but actually contenting himself with the daily paper and an occasional magazine.

'A Sea of Troubles', *The Man with Two Left Feet*, 1917

She had a latent conviction of the immorality of all artists.

The Coming of Bill, 1920

The ordinary man who is paying instalments on the 'Encyclopaedia Britannica' is apt to get over-excited and to skip impatiently to Volume XXVIII (Vet-Zym) to see how it all comes out in the end. Not so Henry. His was not a frivolous mind. He intended to read the 'Encyclopaedia' through, and he was not going to spoil his pleasure by peeping ahead.

'The Man with Two Left Feet', *The Man with Two Left Feet*, 1917

What a girl! He had never in his life before met a woman who could write a letter without a postscript, and this was but the smallest of her unusual gifts.

A Damsel in Distress, 1919

You could tell it was classical music, because the banjo-players were leaning back and chewing gum; and in New York restaurants only death or a classical speciality can stop banjoists.

Uneasy Money, 1917

The years that had passed since Joe had attended the village Sunday School had weakened his once easy familiarity with the characters of the Old Testament.

The Man Upstairs, 1914

It is pretty generally admitted that Geoffrey Chaucer, the eminent poet of the fourteenth century, though obsessed with an almost Rooseveltian passion for the new spelling, was there with the goods when it came to profundity of thought.

'Rough-Hew Them How We Will', *The Man Upstairs*, 1914

. . . a peculiar sort of what-not executed in red mud by an African artist apparently under the influence of trade gin.

Uncle Dynamite, 1948

She could never forget that the man she loved was a man with a past. He had been a poet. Deep down in her soul there was always the corroding fear lest at any moment a particularly fine sunset or the sight of a rose in bud might undo all the work she had done, sending Rodney hot-foot once more to his Thesaurus and rhyming dictionary. It was for this reason that she always hurried him indoors when the sun began to go down and refused to have rose trees in her garden. She was in the same position as a wife who has married a once heavy drinker and, though tolerably certain that he has reformed, nevertheless feels it prudent to tear out the whisky advertisements before giving him his *Tatler*.

'Rodney Has a Relapse', *Nothing Serious*, 1950

'Sir Murgatroyd,' said Mordred formally, 'I have the honour to ask you for your daughter's hand. I am only a poor poet. . . .'

'How poor?' asked the other, keenly.

'The Fiery Wooing of Mordred', *Young Men in Spats*, 1936

It is so easy for a writer of humorous stories to go wrong, as Oliver Wendell Holmes, the *Autocrat At the Breakfast Table* man, once did. He wrote what he knew to be his masterpiece, and in genial mood gave it to his butler to read before taking it down to the editorial office. The butler first giggled a little, then started shaking like a jelly, and finally fell to the floor in convulsions. Holmes had made the mixture too rich. He concludes the poem in which he recorded the incident with the words:

Week after week, both night and day, I nursed that wretched man.
So now I never dare to write as funny as I can.

Preface to *The World of Mr Mulliner*, 1972

'To my daughter Leonora, without whose never-failing sympathy and encouragement this book would have been finished in half the time.'

Dedication of *The Heart of a Goof*, 1926

'Sigsbee Waddington has been a keen supporter of the motion pictures since their inception: and was, I believe, one of the first men in this city to hiss the villain. Whether it was Tom Mix who caused the trouble, or whether his weak intellect was gadually sapped by seeing William S. Hart kiss his horse, I cannot say. But the fact remains that he now yearns for the great open spaces, and if you want to ingratiate yourself with him, all you have to do is to mention that you were born in Iadaho. . . .'
The Small Bachelor, 1927

He decided to go out and grapple with his tragedy in the open air. In novels, he recalled, shepherds tending their flocks on the windswept hills used to be startled by the swift passing of tall, soldierly men with pale, drawn faces, striding through the storm with mouths set like bars of steel, and eyes glittering like flames, staring sightlessly out from under the peaks of their caps. It is one of the defects of London, from the point of view of a man whose heart has just been broken, that it is practically devoid of wild spots in which to stride with a sightless stare.
Bill the Conqueror, 1924

Florence is one of those girls who look on modern enlightened thought as a sort of personal buddy, and receive with ill grace cracks at its expense.
Joy in the Morning, 1947

I could see by the way she sniffed that she was about to become critical. There had always been a strong strain of book-reviewer blood in her.
Aunts Aren't Gentlemen, 1974

In this Victorian novel, Percy has a flowing beard which he appears to have acquired – honestly, one hopes – at the early age of twenty four.
Spring Fever, 1948

Something that Edgar Allan Poe might have written on a rainy Sunday.
Summer Lightning, 1929

A statuette that had been on the mantelpiece, a thing about a foot long with no clothes on . . . Shakespeare it may have been, or Queen Victoria. . . .
The Girl in Blue, 1970

LOVE, MARRIAGE
--- AND ---
SUCH

Bobbie Wickham was a one-girl beauty chorus.
  Jeeves in the Offing, 1960

Even when he ached for Genevieve Bootle, some inner voice told
him that if ever there was a pill it was she. Sometimes the urge to
fold her in his arms and the urge to haul off and slap her over the
nose with a piece of blotting paper came so close together that
it was a mere flick of the coin which prevailed.
  'The Castaways', *Blandings Castle and Elsewhere*, 1935

'Love,' she said, 'seems to pump me full of vitamins. It makes
me feel as if the sun were shining and my hat was right and my
shoes were right and my frock was right and my stockings were
right, and somebody had just left me ten thousand a year.'
  Spring Fever, 1948

He was stoutly opposed to the idea of marrying anyone; but if,
as happens to the best of us, he ever were compelled to perform
the wedding glide, he had always hoped it would be some lady
golf champion who would help him with his putting, and thus,
by bringing his handicap down a notch or two, enable him to
save something from the wreck.
  'Honeysuckle Cottage', *Meet Mr Mulliner*, 1927

In the best and deepest sense of the words, a pippin of a girl.
  Uncle Dynamite, 1948

She had never looked so bright, gay, blooming and beautiful. A
Sultan of the old school, always on the alert for fresh talent for
the harem, would have had no hesitation in instructing his
Vizier to secure her name and telephone number, and would
have been depressed if business had not resulted.
  Do Butlers Burgle Banks?, 1968

'Last night this Englishman was explaining the rules of cricket
to this American girl and answering all her questions on the
subject, and, as he didn't at any point in the proceedings punch

her on the nose, one is entitled to deduce, I consider, that he must be strongly attracted by her.'
Money for Nothing, 1928

Ginger and Magnolia were locked in an embrace so close that it seemed to me that only powerful machinery could unglue them.
Much Obliged, Jeeves, 1971

'He is a chump, you know. That's what I love about him. That and the way his ears wiggle when he gets excited. Chumps always make the best husbands. When you marry, Sally, grab a chump. Tap his forehead first, and if it rings solid, don't hesitate. All the unhappy marriages come from the husband having brains. What good are brains to a man? They only unsettle him.'
The Adventures of Sally, 1922

He and Rosie had always been like a couple of turtle doves, but he knew only too well that when the conditions are right, a female turtle dove can express herself with a vigour which a Caribbean hurricane might envy.
'Leave it to Algy', *A Few Quick Ones*, 1959

The news of our betrothal was conveyed to Sir Watkyn by letter, and I imagine that the dear girl must have hauled up her slacks about me in a way that led me to suppose that what he was getting was a sort of cross between Robert Taylor and Einstein.
The Code of the Woosters, 1938

'Veronica,' said Tipton, 'is just a sweet simple English girl with about as much brain as would make a jay bird fly crooked, and that's the way I want her.'
Galahad at Blandings, 1964

'It's curious how, when you're in love, you yearn to go about doing acts of kindness to everybody. I am bursting with a sort of yeasty benevolence these days, like one of those chaps in Dickens. I very nearly bought you a tie in London, Bertie.'
The Mating Season, 1949

Five minutes before he had been the little friend of all the world and could have stepped straight into a Dickens novel and no questions asked, but now he viewed the human race with a jaundiced eye and could see no future for it.
  Galahad at Blandings, 1964

'He's just at what you might call the dangerous age. Young enough to have preserved that schoolgirl complexion, and old enough to have gotten tired of work and be looking for a rich wife to take him away from it all.'
  Money in the Bank, 1946

He was a chartered accountant, and all chartered accountants have hearts as big as hotels. You think they're engrossed in auditing the half-yearly balance sheets of Miggs, Montague and Murgatroyd, general importers, and all the time they're writing notes to blondes saying 'Tomorrow, one-thirty, same place.'
  Ice in the Bedroom, 1961

There is probably nothing so stimulating to a young fiancé as the knowledge that he has got his story ready and that it will be impossible for the most captious critic to punch holes in it.
  Ice in the Bedroom, 1961

I have made rather a close study of the married state, and I know what happens when one turtle dove gets the goods on the other turtle dove. Bingo Little has often told me that if Mrs Bingo had managed to get on him some of the things that it seemed likely she was going to get, the moon would have been turned to blood and Civilisation shaken to its foundations. I have heard much the same thing from other husbands of my acquaintance, and of course similar upheavals occur when it is the little woman who is caught bending.
  Jeeves and the Feudal Spirit, 1954

I was compelled to remind myself that an English gentleman does not swat a sitting redhead.
  Jeeves in the Offing, 1960

I was in rare fettle and the heart had touched a new high. I don't know anything that braces one up like finding you haven't got to get married after all.
  Jeeves in the Offing, 1960

'You will have to behave like the heroes of those novels which were so popular at one time, who went about in riding breeches and were not above giving the girl of their choice a couple with a hunting-crop on the spot where it would do most good.'
   Uncle Dynamite, 1948

'Mother's idea of a mate for me has always been a well-to-do millionaire or a Duke with a large private income.'
   Jeeves in the Offing, 1960

Veronica Wedge was one of those girls who, if they have not plenty of precious stones on their persons, feel nude.
   Galahad at Blandings, 1964

'He was a regular devil in those days. And look at him now. All dried up like a kippered herring and wouldn't kiss Helen of Troy if you brought her to him asleep in a chair with a sprig of mistletoe suspended over her. That's what comes of being a solicitor, it saps the vital juices. Johnny doesn't even embezzle his clients' money, which I should have thought was about the only fun a solicitor can get out of life.'
   Ice in the Bedroom, 1961

You can't go by what a girl says, when she's giving you hell for making a chump of yourself. It's like Shakespeare. Sounds well but doesn't mean anything.
   Joy in the Morning, 1947

I viewed the situation without concern. To Boko, who had actually been in the ring with the young geezer while she was exploding in all directions, it had naturally seemed that the end of the world had come and Judgment Day set in with unusual severity. But to me, the cool and level-headed bystander, the whole thing had been pure routine. One shrugged the shoulders and recognised it for what it was – viz. pure apple sauce. Love's silken bonds are not broken just because the female half of the sketch takes umbrage at the loony behaviour of the male partner and slips it across him in a series of impassioned speeches. However devoutly a girl may worship the man of her choice, there always comes a time when she feels an irresistible urge to haul off and let him have it in the neck.
   Joy in the Morning, 1947

'Can you dance? ' said the girl.

Lancelot gave a short, amused laugh. He was a man who never let his left hip know what his right hip was doing.

'Came the Dawn', *Meet Mr Mulliner*, 1927

They were some rather special gents' half-hose from the Burlington Arcade, subtly passionate, and he was hoping much from them in his wooing.

'Something Squishy', *Mr Mulliner Speaking*, 1929

'You're too young to marry,' said Mr McKinnon, a stout bachelor.

'So was Methuselah,' said James, a stouter.

'Honeysuckle Cottage', *Meet Mr Mulliner*, 1927

A frightful, tender, melting look, that went through me like a red-hot brad-awl through a pat of butter and filled me with a nameless fear.

Joy in the Morning, 1947

Florence Craye is as imperious as a traffic cop. I felt that Ginger, mistaking it for a peach, had plucked a lemon in the garden of love.

Much Obliged, Jeeves, 1971

A tear stole down her cheek. Jerry, seeing it, writhed with remorse. He realised how a good-hearted executioner at an Oriental court must feel after strangling an odalisque with a bowstring.

Pigs Have Wings, 1952

Veronica Wedge was a girl of a radiant blonde loveliness. Nature had not given her more than about as much brain as would fit comfortably into an aspirin bottle, feeling no doubt that it was better not to overdo the thing, but apart from that she had everything.

Galahad at Blandings, 1964

In her face, it seemed to him, was concentrated all the beauty of all the ages. Confronted with this girl, Cleopatra would have looked like Nellie Wallace, and Helen of Troy might have been her plain sister.

'Came the Dawn', *Meet Mr Mulliner*, 1927

She laughed. Analysing it, Jerry described it to himself as a silvery laugh. Rather like, he thought, for there was a touch of the poet in him, the sound ice makes in a jug of beer on a hot day in August.

The Girl in Blue, 1970

That time when Florence had broken her engagement to me my spirits soared and I went about singing like a relieved nightingale.

Much Obliged, Jeeves, 1971

'Do you love me?'

'Of course I do, my king. When you do that flat-footed Black Bottom step with a sort of wiggly twiggle at the end, I feel as if I were eating plovers' eggs in a new dress to the accompaniment of heavenly music.'

'Came the Dawn', *Meet Mr Mulliner*, 1927

In Aurelia's glorious eye there was a look that he had never seen before, the sort of look Kreisler or somebody like that beholds in the eyes of the front row as he lowers his violin and brushes his forehead with the back of his hand. A look of worship.

'The Reverent Wooing of Archibald', *Mr Mulliner Speaking*, 1929

I had to respect a man capable of turning on Florence like a tiger. I would hardly have thought Attila the Hun could have done it, even at the peak of his form.

Joy in the Morning, 1947

She came clean. I suppose a girl who has been going about for some weeks as sore as a gumboil and with the heart cracked in two places gets to feel that maidenly pride is all very well but what eases the soul is confession.

The Mating Season, 1949

There are girls, few perhaps but to be found if one searches carefully, who when their advice is ignored and disaster ensues, do not say 'I told you so'. Mavis was not of their number.

Pearls, Girls and Monty Bodkin, 1972

He was overcome with astonishment that his son Frederick should have been able to win the heart of a girl so beautiful, so sympathetic, so extraordinarily rich.
'Lord Emsworth Acts for the Best', *Blandings Castle and Elsewhere*, 1935

One of the chief drawbacks to entertaining in your home a girl who has been crossed in love is that she is extremely apt to go about the place doing good. All that life holds for her now is the opportunity of being kind to others, and she intends to be kind if it chokes them. For two weeks Lord Emsworth's beautiful young niece had been moving to and fro through the castle with drawn face, doing good right and left: and his lordship, being handiest, had had to bear the brunt of it.
'Company for Gertrude', *Blandings Castle and Elsewhere*, 1935

He was a man of strong passions, and the green-eyed monster ran up his leg and bit him to the bone.
Full Moon, 1947

'This is blackmail!'
'With the possible exception of diamonds,' said Gladys, 'a girl's best friend.'
'A Good Cigar is a Smoke', *Plum Pie*, 1966

'I'd be crazy to propose to her, but when I see that profile of hers I feel the only thing worth doing in the world is to grab her and start shouting for clergymen and bridesmaids to come running.'
'Life with Freddie', *Plum Pie*, 1966

'My wife tries to drag me to routs and revels from time to time, but I toss my curls at her and refuse to stir. I often think that the ideal life would be to have plenty of tobacco and be cut by the County.'
Uncle Dynamite, 1948

She ignored my observation. Show me a woman, I sometimes say, and I will show you someone who is going to ignore my observations.
Aunts Aren't Gentlemen, 1974

. . . said Gertrude with a significant gnash of the teeth.
Pearls, Girls and Monty Bodkin, 1972

Where one goes wrong when looking for the ideal girl is in making one's selection before walking the full length of the counter.

Much Obliged, Jeeves, 1971

When he had married her, she had been slim and svelte. But she had also been the relict of the late P. Homer Horlick, the Cheese King, and he had left her several million dollars. Most of the interest accruing from this fortune she had, so it seemed to Sigsbee H. Waddington, spent on starchy foods.

The Small Bachelor, 1927

'I suppose I shall have to give my consent, my dear. And here is a piece of advice you will find useful in your married life. Don't watch his eyes. Watch his knees. They will tell you when he is setting himself for a swing. And when he swings, roll with the punch.'

Uncle Fred in the Springtime, 1939

'Angela!' he woofed. 'Don't talk to me about Angela! Angela's a rag and a bone and a hank of hair and an A1 scourge, if you want to know. She gave me the push. Yes, she did. Simply because I had the manly courage to speak out candidly on the subject of that ghastly hat she was chump enough to buy. It made her look like a Peke, and I told her it made her look like a Peke. And instead of admiring me for my fearless honesty she bunged me out on my ear. Faugh!'

'The Ordeal of Young Tuppy', *Very Good, Jeeves*, 1930

Nothing so surely introduces a sour note into a wedding ceremony as the abrupt disappearance of the groom in a cloud of dust.

A Pelican at Blandings, 1969

In the days before he fell under Florence's spell, Ginger was rather apt to get slung out of restaurants for throwing eggs into the electric fan, and he seldom escaped unjugged on Boat Race night for pinching policemen's helmets.

Much Obliged, Jeeves, 1971

After his fiancée has broken the engagement a man feels sombre, if you know what I mean, and unsettled, and rather inclined to read Portuguese Love Sonnets and smoke too much.

Laughing Gas, 1936

As a child of eight Mr Trout had once kissed a girl of six under the mistletoe at a Christmas party, but there his sex life had come to an abrupt halt.
Bachelors Anonymous, 1973

Ernest Plinlimmon was not one of your butterflies who flit from flower to flower. He was an average adjuster, and average adjusters are like chartered accountants. When they love, they give their hearts for ever.
'There's Always Golf', *Lord Emsworth and Others*, 1937

A strange sensation of weakness and humility swept over her. So might the cave woman have felt when, with her back against a cliff and unable to dodge, she watched her suitor take his club in the interlocking grip, and, after a preliminary waggle, start his back swing.
'The Rough Stuff', *The Clicking of Cuthbert*, 1922

A cauliflower ear doesn't matter if it covers a warm heart.
Bachelors Anonymous, 1973

She gazed at me with a tender goggle.
The Code of the Woosters, 1938

Madeline Bassett laughed the tinkling, silvery laugh which was one of the things that had got her so disliked by the better element.
The Code of the Woosters, 1938

You know, the more I see of women, the more I think that there ought to be a law. Something has got to be done about this sex, or the whole fabric of Society will collapse, and then what silly asses we shall all look.
The Code of the Woosters, 1938

'No, Ronnie. It's nice of you to try to cheer me up. But I regard the entire personnel of the ensembles of our musical comedy theatres as – if you will forgive me being Victorian for a moment – painted hussies.'
   'They've got to paint.'
   'Well, they needn't huss. And they needn't ensnare my son.'
   Heavy Weather, 1933

I am a man who can read faces, and Chuffy's had seemed to me highly suggestive. Not only had its expression, as he spoke of Pauline, been that of a stuffed frog with a touch of the Soul's Awakening about it, but it had also turned a fairly deepish crimson in colour. The tip of the nose had wiggled, and there had been embarrassment in the manner. The result being that I had become firmly convinced that the old schoolmate had copped it properly and was in love.

Thank You, Jeeves, 1934

The odd noise he was making I could diagnose, not as the love call which she appeared to think it, but as the stern and censorious gruffle of a man who, finding his loved one on alien premises in heliotrope pyjamas, is stricken to the core, cut to the quick and as sore as a gumboil.

Thank You, Jeeves, 1934

Gussie had bunged his heart at her feet; she had picked it up, and, almost immediately after doing so, had discovered that he had been stewed to the eyebrows all the time. No girl likes to feel that a chap has got to be thoroughly plastered before he can ask her to marry him. It wounds the pride.

Right Ho, Jeeves, 1934

Dinty took over the conduct of affairs with the quiet, efficient smoothness so characteristic of women when they are about to embark on a course of action not scrupulously honest.

Barmy in Wonderland, 1952

Tuppy's manifest pippedness excited my compash, and I ventured a kindly word. 'I don't suppose you know what *au pied de la lettre* means, Tuppy, but that's how I don't think you ought to take all that stuff Angela was saying just now too much.'

Right Ho, Jeeves, 1934

'Well, look at Jael, the wife of Heber. Dug spikes into the guest's coco-nut while he was asleep, and then went swanking about the place like a Girl Guide. No wonder they say "Oh, woman, woman!" '

'Who?'

'The chaps who do.'

Right Ho, Jeeves, 1934

Few things in life are more embarrassing than the necessity of having to inform an old friend that you have just got engaged to his fiancée.
Big Money, 1931

'We just happened to be sitting in a cemetery, and I asked her how she would like to see my name on her tombstone.'
If I Were You, 1931

Much as he worshipped the girl, he sometimes thought she must have governess blood in her.
Hot Water, 1932

So remarkable was this girl's loveliness that Mr Gedge momentarily forgot his troubles and unconsciously straightened his tie. House-broken husband though he was, he still had an eye for beauty.
Hot Water, 1932

She frowned. As she frowned, she tapped her foot. And as she tapped her foot, she said 'H'm!' And she meant it, too.
Hot Water, 1932

What magic there is in a girl's smile. It is the raisin which, dropped in the yeast of male complacency, induces fermentation.
The Girl on the Boat, 1922

'It's got so nowadays,' said Ukridge, with a strong sense of injury, 'that you've only to throw a girl a kindly word, and the next thing you know you're in the Lord Warden Hotel at Dover, picking the rice out of your hair.'
'No Wedding Bells for Him', *Ukridge*, 1924

Now, seeing her weeping and broken before him, with all the infernal cheek he so deprecated swept away on a wave of woe, his heart softened. It has been a matter of speculation among historians what Wellington would have done if Napoleon had cried at Waterloo.
Sam the Sudden, 1925

Woman's intuition is a wonderful thing. There was probably not an alienist in the land who, having listened so far, would not have sprung at George and held him down with one hand while with the other he signed the necessary certificate of lunacy. But Molly Waddington saw deeper into the matter. She was touched. This was love.
The Small Bachelor, 1927

She was not normally an unkind girl but the impulse of the female of the species to torture the man it loves is well known. Women may be ministering angels when pain and anguish wring the brow: but if at other times she sees a chance to prod the loved one and watch him squirm, she hates to miss it.
The Small Bachelor, 1927

There had been a period when, he being fifteen and she ten, Pat had lavished on him all the worship of a small girl for a big boy who can wiggle his ears and is not afraid of cows. But since then her attitude had changed. Her manner towards him nowadays alternated between that of a nurse towards a child who is not quite right in the head and that of the owner of a clumsy but rather likeable dog.
Money for Nothing, 1928

'Molly!'
'Yes, mother?'
Mrs Waddington was frowning as she entered the room. How often she had told this girl to call her 'mater'!
The Small Bachelor, 1927

It is a curious fact, and one frequently noted by philosophers, that every woman in the world cherishes within herself a deep-rooted belief, from which nothing can shake her, that the particular man to whom she has plighted her love is to be held personally blameworthy for practically all of the untoward happenings of life.
Sam the Sudden, 1925

There was all heaven in Anne Benedick's laugh. It conjured up visions of a cosy house on a winter's night, with one's slippers on one's feet, the dog on one's lap, an open fire in the grate and the good old pipe drawing nicely.
Money in the Bank, 1946

The late Mr Ford had spent most of his married life either quarrelling with or separated from his wife, but since death he had been canonised as 'poor dear Elmer'.
Piccadilly Jim, 1918

There are men who fear repartee in a wife more keenly than a sword.
Jill the Reckless, 1921

Gally in his younger days had never been happier than when knee-deep in barmaids and ballet girls.
Pigs Have Wings, 1952

Nothing tends to cool the human heart more swiftly than babytalk.
Jeeves in the Offing, 1960

Barmy's open, engaging face had aroused the maternal instinct in her. Even when eyeing him with the same hard intentness with which Jack Dempsey used to regard his opponents in the ring, she was conscious of a strong impulse to stroke his nose.
Barmy in Wonderland, 1952

'I attribute my whole success in life to a rigid observance of the fundamental rule – Never have yourself tattooed with any woman's name, not even her initials.'
French Leave, 1956

He was after her money. They're all the same, these effete aristocrats of the old country. Make a noise like a rich widow anywhere in England, and out come all the Dukes and Earls and Viscounts, howling like wolves.
Ring for Jeeves, 1953

The years had dealt lightly with the erstwhile Maudie Montrose. A little more matronly, perhaps, than the girl with the hourglass figure who had played the St Bernard dog to the thirsty wayfarers at the old Criterion, she still made a distinct impression on the eye, and the landlord of the Emsworth Arms, his growing son Percy and half a dozen Shropshire lads who were propping up the establishment's outer wall had stamped her with the seal of their popeyed approval.

'It's astonishing,' said Gally. 'One gasps. Put you in a bathing suit, add you to the list of contestants in any seaside beauty competition, and you would still have the judges whooping and blowing kisses and asking you if you were doing anything next Saturday night.'

Pigs Have Wings, 1952

'I turned him down like a bedspread.'

'The Right Approach', *A Few Quick Ones*, 1959

When last seen he had had all the earmarks of one about whom Love had twined its silken fetters. Dash it, you don't go telling people you will break their spines in four places unless you have more than a passing fancy for the bally girl. So what had occurred to dim the lamp of love and all that sort of thing?

Jeeves and the Feudal Spirit, 1954

She made one of those foolish remarks which do so much to confirm a man in his conviction that women as a sex should be suppressed.

Joy in the Morning, 1947

'I taught him to ski,' said Bobbie, a dreamy look coming into her twin starlikes. 'I shall never forget the day I helped him unscramble himself after he had taken a toss on the beginners' slope. He had both legs wrapped round his neck. I think that is when love dawned. My heart melted as I sorted him out.'

Jeeves in the Offing, 1960

Soapy Molloy was devouring Dolly with adoring eyes. Few more loving husbands than he had ever cracked rocks in Sing Sing.

Ice in the Bedroom, 1961

At the sight of that ashen face the haughtiness went out of Roberta Wickham with a whoosh, to be replaced by all the old love, sympathy, womanly tenderness and what not and she bounded at him like a leopardess getting together with a lost cub. . . . She was, in fact, melted by his distress, as so often happens with the female sex.

Jeeves in the Offing, 1960

'Use your bean, Uncle Fred. You know what you do when your girl gives you the push. You dash off and propose to another girl, just to show her she isn't the only onion in the stew.'

Lord Ickenham nodded. It was many years since he had acted in the manner described, but he, too, had lived in Arcady.

'Ah, youth, youth!' he was saying to himself, and he shuddered a little as he recalled the fearful female down Greenwich Village way, all beads and bangles and matted hair, at whose sandalled feet he had laid his heart the second time Pongo's Aunt Jane had severed relations with him.
Service with a Smile, 1962

'You patted her lunch-hook.'
'Sure I patted her lunch-hook. And why? Because I was trying to sell her oil-stock.'
Money in the Bank, 1946

Any male turtle dove will tell you that, if conditions are right, the female turtle dove can spit on her hands and throw her weight about like Donald Duck.
'The Editor Regrets', *Eggs, Beans and Crumpets*, 1940

A girl may scorn and loathe the scrum-half who leaps at her in rhododendron walks, but let her behold that scrum-half weltering in his blood after being rapped over the head with a tobacco jar, and hate becomes pity, pity forgiveness, and forgiveness love.
Money in the Bank, 1946

'The idea of being united to Madeline Bassett in the bonds of holy wedlock is one that freezes the gizzard. There are certain females whom one respects, admires, reveres, but only from a distance. If they show any signs of attempting to come closer, one is prepared to fight them off with a blackjack. It is to this group that your cousin Madeline belongs.'
The Code of the Woosters, 1938

She stopped me with a pleading yowl.
Code of the Woosters, 1938

A sudden yowl of ecstasy broke from the young pimple.
The Code of the Woosters, 1938

Pongo spoke a little huskily, for he had once more fallen in love at first sight.
Uncle Fred in the Springtime, 1939

The whole wheeze in married life, Bingo had come to learn, was to give the opposite number as few opportunities of saying 'Oh, how could you?' as possible.

'Sonny Boy', *Eggs, Beans and Crumpets*, 1940

While still vague as to what exactly were the qualities he demanded of a wife, he was very clear in his mind that she must not be the sort of girl who routs a man out at midnight to go and pinch portraits and gets him bitten in the leg by Pekinese.

Quick Service, 1940

She spoke so quietly, so meekly, her whole air so like that of a good little girl remorseful for having been naughty, that a wiser and more experienced man than Lionel Green would have climbed the wall and pulled it up after him.

Money in the Bank, 1946

She was a woman capable of checking a charging rhinoceros with a raised eyebrow and a well-bred stare, but she had her softer side.

Money in the Bank, 1946

'He does that sort of thing automatically. Where you or I would light a cigarette and throw off an epigram, Pongo kisses the housemaid. It means nothing. A purely unconscious reflex action.'

Uncle Dynamite, 1948

'I'm going to forgive him the day after tomorrow,' she said. 'Not earlier, because we must have discipline.'

The Mating Season, 1949

Agnes was perhaps a hard judge, but Cora McGuffy Spottsworth looked to her like the sort of woman who goes about stealing the plans of forts – or, at the best, leaning back negligently and saying 'Prince, my fan.' The impression Agnes formed was of something that might be all right stepping out of a pie at a bachelor party, but not the type you could take home to meet mother.

'Feet of Clay', *Nothing Serious*, 1950

Warm though the morning was, he shivered, as only a confirmed bachelor gazing into the naked face of matrimony can shiver.

The Old Reliable, 1951

His eyes were rolling in their sockets, and his face had taken on the colour and expression of a devout tomato. I could see that he loved her like a thousand of bricks.
Joy in the Morning, 1947

He snorted devoutly.
'Excelsior', *Nothing Serious*, 1950

In this Cheesewright, it was plain, I had run up against one of those touchy lovers who go about the place in a suspicious and red-eyed spirit, eager to hammer the stuffing out of such of the citizenry as they suppose to be or to have been in any sense matey with the adored object.
Joy in the Morning, 1947

Joss was still kissing Sally, and Sally, who in the opening stages had kicked him on the shin, had just begun to realise that she was feeling disgracefully happy about it all.
Quick Service, 1940

Love, he felt, and he was a man who had thought about these things, should not manifest itself in such a strongly marked inclination, when in the presence of the adored object, to stand on one leg and twiddle the fingers.
Money in the Bank, 1946

The laughing Love God has been properly up on his toes. Never an idle moment. Day and night shifts.
Joy in the Morning, 1947

Young Bingo shot a glance of such succulent devotion at her that I reeled in my tracks.
'Comrade Bingo', *The Inimitable Jeeves*, 1923

'Are wives always like that, Jeeves? I mean, welcoming criticism of the lord and master?'
'They are generally open to suggestions from the outside public with regard to the improvement of their husbands, sir.'
'That is why married men are wan, what?'
'Yes, sir.'
'Jeeves and the Old School Chum', *Very Good, Jeeves*, 1930

Like so many of these big muscle-bound men, he was a mere serf in the home.

'The Letter of the Law', *Lord Emsworth and Others*, 1937

'Sorry to call you up at this hour. But will you marry me?'
'Certainly. Who is that?'
'Smallwood Bessemer.'

'Tangled Hearts', *Nothing Serious*, 1950

She was now in excellent fettle – as radiant and happy as only a redhaired girl who enjoys emotional quarrelling can be after a thoroughly invigorating turn-up. Life, to be really life for her, had to consist of a series of devastating rows and terrific reconciliations. Anything milder she considered insipid. Lotus Blossom had been born a Murphy of Hoboken, and all the Hoboken Murphys were like that.

The Luck of the Bodkins, 1935

'I think a girl's right to put a stick of dynamite underneath the loved one every now and then, when he gets above himself, don't you? Her dignity demands it. This makes the third time I've broken the engagement. The first was forty three seconds after I said I would marry him. I guess that's a record. European, anyway. Yessir, forty three seconds after I said I'd marry him I broke the engagement because he took a swing at Wilfred, my little alligator. I held Wilfred up to his face and said "Kiss papa," and Ambrose gave a sort of horrible gurgle and knocked him out of my hands. Imagine! Might have cracked him.'

The Luck of the Bodkins, 1935

One of the things that being engaged does to you is to fill you to the gills with a sort of knightly chivalry. You go about the place like a Boy Scout, pouncing out on passers-by and doing acts of kindness to them.

'Fate', *Young Men in Spats*, 1936

Women are divided broadly into two classes – those who, when jilted, merely drop a silent tear and those who take a niblick from their bag and chase the faithless swain across country with it. It was to this latter section that Agnes Flack belonged. Attila the Hun might have broken off his engagement to her, but nobody except Attila the Hun, and he only on one of his best mornings.

'Scratch Man', *A Few Quick Ones*, 1959

'I said that I loved her as no one had ever loved before. Upon which, she said that I did not love her as much as she loved me. I said yes, I did, because my love stood alone. She said no, it didn't, because hers did. I said it couldn't because mine did. Hot words ensued, and a few moments later she was saying that she never wanted to see or speak to me again, because I was an obstinate, fatheaded son of an Army mule. She then handed back my letters and left me.'
   'The Letter of the Law', *Lord Emsworth and Others*, 1937

Though he scorned and loathed her, he was annoyed to discover that he loved her still. He would have liked to bounce a brick on Prudence Whittaker's head, and yet, at the same time, he would have liked – rather better, as a matter of fact – to crush her to him and cover her face with burning kisses. The whole situation was very complex.
   Summer Moonshine, 1938

Lady Constance was smiling brightly, as women so often do when they are in the process of slipping something raw over their nearest and dearest.
   'The Crime Wave at Blandings', *Lord Emsworth and Others*, 1937

He had studied Woman, and he knew that when Woman gets into a tight place her first act is to shovel the blame off onto the nearest male.
   'Trouble Down at Tudsleigh', *Young Men in Spats*, 1936

'I've often wondered about that scarlet woman. Was she scarlet all over, or was it just that her face was red?'
   The Mating Season, 1949

The exquisite code of politeness of the Woosters prevented me clipping her one on the ear-hole.
   Right Ho, Jeeves, 1934

Hypatia, like all girls who intend to be good wives, made it a practice to look on any suggestions thrown out by her future lord and master as fatuous and futile.

'Gala Night', *Mulliner Nights*, 1933

Nothing so braces a young man in love as the consciousness of having successfully resisted a Tempter who has tried to lure him into a course of action of which the adored object would not approve: and as he recalled the splendid firmness with which he had tied the can to his Uncle Fred's suggestion of a pleasant and instructive afternoon in London, Pongo felt spiritually uplifted.

Uncle Dynamite, 1948

'The great thing is to get the young blighter Pongo safely married and settled down, thus avoiding the risk of his coming in one day and laying on the mat something with a platinum head and an Oxford accent which he picked up on the pier at Blackpool.'

Uncle Dynamite, 1948

Bingo had tried to touch P. P. Purkiss for an advance of salary, but P. P. Purkiss had said it was foreign to the policy of *Wee Tots* to brass up in advance. It really began to look as if he would be forced to the last awful extreme of biting Mrs Bingo's ear, which would mean that he might hear the last of it somewhere round about the afternoon of their golden wedding day, but scarcely before then.

'The Shadow Passes', *Nothing Serious*, 1950

The male sex is divided into rabbits and non-rabbits and the female sex into dashers and doormice.

Jeeves in the Offing, 1960

BUTLERS, VALETS
— AND OTHER —
MENSERVANTS

Beach the butler was a man who had made two chins grow where only one had been before, and his waistcoat swelled like the sail of a racing yacht.
Galahad at Blandings, 1965

'You mustn't take it to heart, Beach, if the boy calls you fat. Admittedly you get your money's worth out of a weighing machine and if your body were fished out of the Thames it would be described as that of a well-nourished man of middle age. But what of it?'
Galahad at Blandings, 1965

The valet withdrew like a duke leaving the Royal Presence, not actually walking backwards but giving the impression of doing so.
The Girl on the Boat, 1922

As a butler Beach deplored Mr Galahad's habit of gossiping with the domestic staff, but as a man he simply loved it.
A Pelican at Blandings, 1969

Jeeves's Uncle Charles Silversmith, the butler at Deverill Hall, was something special. He looked like one of those steel engravings of nineteenth-century statesmen. He had a large, bald head and pale, protruding gooseberry eyes, and those eyes, resting on mine, heightened the Dark Tower feeling considerably. The thought crossed my mind that if something like this had popped out at Childe Roland, he would have clapped spurs to his charger and been off like a jack-rabbit.
The Mating Season, 1949

The butler was looking nervous, like Macbeth interviewing Lady Macbeth after one of her visits to the spare room.
'Buried Treasure', *Lord Emsworth and Others*, 1937

As always when he had solid thinking to do, he made his way to the cell-like seclusion of his pantry. The servants' hall, with its flow of merry quip and flashing badinage, he reserved for his more convivial moments when he was in the mood for the gay whirl. He poured himself out a glass of port, and sat down to ponder.

Quick Service, 1940

I have met many butlers who behaved unexpectedly in their spare time. One I knew played the fiddle; another preached Socialism in Hyde Park. But I had never yet come across a butler who fired pistols.

The Little Nugget, 1913

Silversmith the butler entered left, and I was amazed to see that there was an indulgent smile on his face. It is true that he switched it off immediately and resumed his customary aspect of a respectful chunk of dough, but the facial contortion had undoubtedly been there.

The Mating Season, 1949

It is a very impoverished butler in Beverly Hills who does not own his natty little roadster.

The Old Reliable, 1951

Penny's had been a sheltered life, and she had never before seen a butler with the heeby-jeebies.

Pigs Have Wings, 1952

'Yes, sir,' said Jeeves in a low, cold voice, as if he had been bitten in the leg by a personal friend.

'Clustering Round Young Bingo', *Carry On, Jeeves*, 1925

I was dashed if I was going to let Jeeves treat me like a bally one-man chain-gang.

'Jeeves and the Unbidden Guest', *Carry On, Jeeves*, 1925

I trod on the starter and we began the journey, Jeeves standing on the pavement, seeing us off like an archbishop blessing pilgrims, his air that of one who would shortly be following by train with the heavy luggage.

Joy in the Morning, 1947

'My dear Smedley, you can't stick lighted matches between the toes of an English butler. He would raise his eyebrows and freeze you with a glance. You'd feel as if he had caught you using the wrong fork.'

The Old Reliable, 1951

Bowles, like all proprietors of furnished rooms in the Sloane Square neighbourhood, is an ex-butler, and even in a plaid dressing gown he retained much of the cold majesty which so intimidated me by day.

'The Masked Troubadour', *Lord Emsworth and Others*, 1937

'We had a butler called Blenkinsop in those days, and he reported Reggie to father for stealing jam, and father beat Reggie, and Reggie went out and wrote "Death to Harold Blenkinsop" on all the walls in white chalk. Blenkinsop was very annoyed about it. He said it would weaken his authority with the lower domestics, especially as he had always been most careful to keep it from them that his name was Harold.'

The Luck of the Bodkins, 1935

Blizzard was of the fine old school of butlers. Before coming to the Fisher home he had been for fifteen years in the service of an earl, and his appearance suggested that throughout those fifteen years he had not let a day pass without its pint of port. He radiated port and pop-eyed dignity. He had splay feet and three chins, and when he walked his curving waistcoat preceded him like the advance guard of some royal procession.

'High Stakes', *The Heart of a Goof*, 1926

'What do we feed a butler on?'
'Oh, anything you have yourselves. Put sulphur in his port in hot weather.'

'High Stakes', *The Heart of a Goof*, 1926

'What-ho, Jeeves!' I said, entering the room where he waded knee-deep in suitcases and shirts and winter suitings, like a sea-beast among rocks. 'Packing?'

'Yes, sir,' replied the honest fellow, for there are no secrets between us.

'The Ordeal of Young Tuppy', *Very Good, Jeeves*, 1930

It was the soft cough of Jeeves's which always reminds me of a very old sheep clearing its throat on a distant mountain top.

Stiff Upper Lip, Jeeves, 1963

Jeeves lugged my purple socks out of the drawer as if he were a vegetarian fishing a caterpillar out of his salad.

'Jeeves and the Chump Cyril', *My Man Jeeves*, 1919

Oakshott was one of those stout, impressive, ecclesiastical butlers. A man with a presence. Meeting him in the street and ignoring the foul bowler hat he wore on his walks abroad, you would have put him down as a Bishop in mufti or, at least, a plenipotentiary at one of the better courts.

'The Come-Back of Battling Billson', *Lord Emsworth and Others*, 1937

In private life butlers relax that impassive gravity which the rules of their union compel them to maintain in public. Spring something sensational on a butler when he is chatting with you in your bedroom, and he will leap and goggle like any ordinary man. Phipps did so now.

'Buried Treasure', *Lord Emsworth and Others*, 1937

Ice formed on the butler's upper slopes.

Pigs Have Wings, 1952

'I found Oakshott in his pantry,' said Ukridge. 'Dismissing with a gesture the housemaid who was sitting on his knee, I unfolded my proposition.'

'Success Story', *Nothing Serious*, 1950

The great door of the castle closed with a soft but significant bang – as doors closed when handled by an untipped butler.

Leave it to Psmith, 1923

Any man under thirty years of age who tells you he is not afraid of an English butler lies.

'The Good Angel', *The Man Upstairs*, 1914

'My God! If a butler publicly rebuked me I think I should commit suicide. I couldn't survive it. I don't suppose there is anything so terrible as a snub from a butler.'
Something Fresh, 1915

A vintage butler of obviously a very good year.
Something Fishy, 1957

Nothing, except possibly the discovery that the ground on which she treads is worshipped by a butler for whom she has long entertained feelings deeper and warmer than those of ordinary friendship, can raise a woman's spirits more than the knowledge that the brother who is the apple of her eye is, in spite of appearance, in full possession of his marbles. One can understand Phoebe Wisdom humming a light air. A weaker woman would have sung.
Cocktail Time, 1958

For some reason, probably known to scientists, butlers, as far at any rate as outward appearance is concerned, do not grow old as we grow old. Keggs, reclining in his chair with his feet on a footstool and a mild cigar between his lips, looked almost precisely as he had looked a quarter of a century ago. Then he had resembled a Roman emperor who had been doing himself too well on starchy foods. His aspect now was of a slightly stouter Roman emperor, one who had given up any attempt to watch his calories and liked his potatoes with lots of butter on them.
Something Fishy, 1959

Jeeves entered – or perhaps one should say shimmered into – the room . . . tall and dark and impressive. He might have been one of the better class ambassadors or the youngish High Priest of some refined and dignified religion.
Ring for Jeeves, 1953

This Binstead was one of those young, sprightly butlers, encountering whom one feels that in the deepest and holiest sense they are not butlers at all, but merely glorified footmen.
Pigs Have Wings, 1952

Bulstrode, Mrs C. Hamilton Brimble's English butler, had heard noises in the night, and when English butlers hear noises in the night, they act.
Barmy in Wonderland, 1952

'If butlers come can port be far behind?'
'Success Story', *Nothing Serious*, 1950

Parker made no comment. He stood in the doorway, trying to look as like a piece of furniture as possible – which is the duty of a good butler.
The Pothunters, 1902

One of the rummy things about Jeeves is that, unless you watch like a hawk, you very seldom see him come into a room. He's like one of those weird birds in India who dissolve themselves into thin air and nip through space in a sort of disembodied way and assemble the parts again just where they want them. I've got a cousin who's what they call a Theosophist, and he says he's often nearly worked the thing himself, but couldn't quite bring it off, probably owing to having fed in his boyhood on the flesh of animals slain in anger and pie.
'The Artistic Career of Corky', *Carry On, Jeeves*, 1925

When Sturgis spoke, it was in a lowered voice, which gave his delivery the effect of a sheep bleating with cotton-wool in its mouth.
Money for Nothing, 1928

Mrs Waddington's eye blazed imperiously upon the butler. He met it with the easy aplomb of one who in his time has looked at dukes and made them feel that their trousers were bagging at the knees.
The Small Bachelor, 1927

'I have no desire to be a deputy,' said the butler, with the cold subtinkle in his voice which had once made the younger son of a marquess resign from his clubs and go to Uganda.
The Small Bachelor, 1927

Just because this fine old man had one of those mild, goofy faces and bleated like a sheep when he talked, John had dismissed him without further thought as a dodderer. . . . But now. . . . There is no known case on record of a man patting a butler on the head, but John at this moment came very near to providing one.
Money for Nothing, 1928

The world may be divided broadly into two classes – men who will believe you when you suddenly inform them at half-past eleven on a summer morning that you propose to start making

rabbit-hutches, and men who will not. Sturgis the butler looked as if he belonged to the former and far more likeable class. He looked, indeed, like a man who would believe anything.
Money for Nothing, 1928

Bowles was an ex-butler, and about him, as about all ex-butlers, there clung like a garment an aura of dignified superiority which had never failed to crush my spirit.
'Ukridge's Dog College', *Ukridge*, 1924

In the hall the valet was tapping the barometer with the wrist action of an ambassador knocking on the door of a friendly monarch.
The Girl on the Boat, 1922

Mr Bennett rang the bell, and presently there entered a grave, thin, intellectual-looking man who looked like a duke, only more respectable. This was Webster, Mr Bennett's valet.
The Girl on the Boat, 1922

Slingsby loomed in the doorway like a dignified cloudbank.
If I Were You, 1931

Beach's bullfinch continued to chirp reflectively to itself, like a man trying to remember a tune in his bath.
Summer Lightning, 1929

He felt more like a gay young footman than a butler of years' standing.
Summer Lightning, 1929

There are aspects of Jeeves's character which have frequently caused coldness to arise between us. He is one of those fellows who, if you give them a thingummy, take a what-d'you-call-it. His work is often raw, and he has been known to refer to me as 'mentally negligible'. More than once it has been my painful duty to squelch in him a tendency to get uppish and treat the young master like a serf or peon. These are grave defects. But one thing I have never failed to hand the man. He is magnetic. There is about him something that seems to soothe and hypnotise. To the best of my knowledge he has never encountered a charging rhinoceros, but should the contingency occur, I have no doubt that the animal, meeting his eye, would check itself in mid-stride, roll over and lie purring with its legs in the air.
Right Ho, Jeeves, 1934

'Jeeves,' I said, and I am free to admit that in my emotion I bleated like a lamb drawing itself to the attention of the parent sheep.
Right Ho, Jeeves, 1934

Words like '*marmiton de Domange*', '*pigneuf*', '*hurluberlu*', and '*roustisseur*' were fluttering from Anatole the chef like bats out of a barn.
Right Ho, Jeeves, 1934

I must say I can't see why Jeeves shouldn't go down in legend and song. Daniel did, on the strength of putting in half an hour or so in the lions' den and leaving the dumb chums in a condition of suavity and *camaraderie*; and if what Jeeves had just done wasn't entitled to rank well above a feat like that, I'm no judge of form. In less than five minutes he had reduced this ravening Stoker from a sort of human wildcat to a positive domestic pet.
Thank You, Jeeves, 1934

I remember Jeeves saying to me once, apropos of how you can never tell what the weather's going to do, that full many a glorious morning had he seen flatter the mountain tops with sovereign eye and then turn into a rather nasty afternoon.
The Code of the Woosters, 1938

'The entire question of butlers, Corky, is one that wants thoroughly threshing out. How do they do it? Wherein consists their mystic spell? What is this magnetism in them that subdues the proudest? You would have thought a barmaid, accustomed to mixing whisky-and-splashes for the highest in the land – for the clientele of the Blue Anchor is notoriously exclusive and numbers in its ranks people like shop-walkers from Harrods and sergeants in the Guards – would have been proof against it. But no. One glance from those bulbous eyes had reduced Flossie to a blushing pulp.'
'The Come-Back of Battling Billson', *Lord Emsworth and Others*, 1937

'I found that Vosper was willing to come to America. He had been butler for eighteen years with the Duke, and he told me that he couldn't stand the sight of the back of his head any longer.'
'High Stakes', *The Heart of a Goof*, 1926

'Jeeves, do you always carry Mickey Finns on you?'
... 'I am seldom without a small supply, Madam. . . .
Opportunities for their use are constantly arising.'
Much Obliged, Jeeves, 1971

He had once been Ginger Winship's valet.
'Nice enough young fellow he always seemed to me, though
the wrong size.'
'Wrong size?'
'His shirts didn't fit me. . . .'
Much Obliged, Jeeves, 1971

'I don't actually love my butler Coggs. A distant affection,
rather tempered with awe,' said Lord Ickenham.
Uncle Dynamite, 1948

If Beach were surprised at the presence of the younger son of the
house in the amber drawing-room with a sack of rats in his
hand, he gave no indication of the fact. With a murmured
apology, he secured the sack and started to withdraw. It was
not, strictly, his place to carry rats, but a good butler is always
ready to give and take. Only so can the amenities of a large
country house be preserved.
'The Go-Getter', *Blandings Castle and Elsewhere*, 1935

He looked at it with distaste, like a butler
inspecting a bottle of wine of an inferior
vintage.
Spring Fever, 1948

Jeeves let his brain out another notch.
The Mating Season, 1949

Spink the butler withdrew, gracefully and sinuously, with a
touch of the smugness of an ambassador who is pluming himself
on having delivered the important despatches without dropping
them.
Spring Fever, 1948

Jeeves doesn't exactly smile on these occasions, because he
never does, but the lips twitch slightly at the corners and the eye
is benevolent.
Joy in the Morning, 1947

The butler increased the detached expression which good butlers wear on these occasions. He looked like a prominent banker refusing to speak without advice of counsel.

'The Voice from the Past', *Mulliner Nights*, 1933

The head gardener was standing gazing at the moss like a high priest of some ancient religion about to stick the gaff into the human sacrifice.

'Lord Emsworth and the Girl Friend', *Blandings Castle and Elsewhere*, 1935

It is only an exceptionally mild and easy-tempered man who can receive with equanimity the news that his sister will shortly be taking for better or worse a butler who has recently locked him in the wine-cellar.

Cocktail Time, 1958

'Phoebe's marrying a butler!'

'Someone's got to, or the race of butlers would die out.'

Cocktail Time, 1958

Jerry had never been snubbed by a butler before, and the novel experience made him feel as if he had been walking in the garden in the twilight and had stepped on a rake and had the handle jump up and hit him on the tip of the nose.

Pigs Have Wings, 1952

In times of domestic crisis, Jeeves has the gift of creating the illusion that he is not there.

Ring for Jeeves, 1953

Though not often given to theological speculation, he was wondering why Providence, if obliged to make head gardeners, had found it necessary to make them so Scotch. . . . all the ingredients of a first class mule simply thrown away.

'Lord Emsworth and the Girl Friend', *Blandings Castle and Elsewhere*, 1935

GOLF

It was a morning when all nature shouted 'Fore!'. The breeze, as it blew gently up from the valley, seemed to bring a message of hope and cheer, whispering of chip-shots holed and brassies landing squarely on the meat.

'The Heart of a Goof', *The Heart of a Goof*, 1926

The clubhouse had broken out into an eruption of roses, smilax, Chinese lanterns, gold-toothed saxophonists, giggling girls and light refreshments. An inhabitant of ancient Babylon would have beamed approvingly on the spectacle, but it made Angus McTavish sick. His idea of a clubhouse was a sort of cathedral filled with serious-minded men telling one another in quiet undertones how they got a four on the long fifteenth.

'Farewell to Legs', *Lord Emsworth and Others*, 1937

On the short fourteenth she got one of those lucky twos which, as James Braid once said to J. H. Taylor, seem like a dome of many-coloured glass to stain the white radiance of Eternity.

'Farewell to Legs', *Lord Emsworth and Others*, 1937

'After all, golf is only a game,' said Millicent.

Women say these things without thinking. It does not mean that there is any kink in their character. They simply don't realise what they are saying.

'Ordeal by Golf', *The Clicking of Cuthbert*, 1922

I attribute the insane arrogance of the later Roman emperors almost entirely to the fact that, never having played golf, they never knew that strange chastening humility which is engendered by a topped chip-shot. If Cleopatra had been outed in the first round of the Ladies' Singles, we should have heard a lot less of her proud imperiousness.

'The Magic Plus-Fours', *The Heart of a Goof*, 1926

Reggie was a troubled spirit these days. He was in love, and he had developed a bad slice with his mid-iron. He was practically a soul in torment.
    A Damsel in Distress, 1919

Cora McGuffy Spotsworth still looked like one of those women who lure men's souls to the shoals of sin, but there was no question that, as far as knowing what to do with a good number four iron when you put it into her hands was concerned, she would make a good wife.
    'Feet of Clay', *Nothing Serious*, 1950

I have said that George Porter's head was bowed, but his trouble was that he did not keep it bowed. Too often, when making a shot, he would raise it heavenwards, as if asking why a good man should be persecuted like this, which of course resulted in topping.
    'Joy Bells for Walter', *A Few Quick Ones*, 1959

Mere dregs of the golfing world who enter competitions for the hell of the thing or because they know they look well in sports clothes.
    'Feet of Clay', *Nothing Serious*, 1950

Cora McGuffy Spotsworth might, and probably would, recline on tiger skins in the nude and expect Sidney to drink champagne out of her shoes, but she would never wear high heels on the links or say Tee Hee when she missed a putt.
    'Feet of Clay', *Nothing Serious*, 1950

George Mackintosh was a handsome, well set-up man, with no vices except a tendency to use the mashie for shots which should have been made with the light iron. He never swayed his body, moved his head, or pressed. He was always ready to utter a tactful grunt when an opponent foozled. And when he himself achieved a glaring fluke, his self-reproachful click of the tongue was music to his adversary's bruised soul.
    'The Salvation of George Mackintosh', *The Clicking of Cuthbert*, 1922

I saw that Anastatia had buried her face in her hands, while William, with brotherly solicitude, stood scratching the top of her head with a number three iron, no doubt in a well-meant effort to comfort and console.
    'Rodney Has a Relapse', *Nothing Serious*, 1950

Walter clasped her to his bosom, using the interlocking grip.
  'Joy Bells for Walter', *A Few Quick Ones*, 1959

Agnes Flack was the undisputed female champion of the club. She had the shoulders of an all-in wrestler, the breezy self-confidence of a sergeant-major and a voice like a toastmaster's. I have often seen the Wrecking Crew, that quartette of spavined septuagenarian golfers whose pride it was that they never let anyone through, scatter like leaves in an autumn gale at the sound of her stentorian 'Fore!'.
  'Scratch Man', *A Few Quick Ones*, 1959

Mr Bunting suggested that Lord Tilbury should arm himself with something solid from the bag of golf clubs which was standing in the corner of the room. He recommended the niblick. Lord Tilbury felt that it was a wise choice. He had had no previous experience of intimidating a burglar, but instinct told him that it was a niblick shot.
  Frozen Assets, 1964

Her hair was a deep chestnut, her eyes blue, her nose small and laid back with about as much loft as a light iron.
  'Chester Forgets Himself', *The Heart of a Goof*, 1926

It is an excellent thing that women should be encouraged to take up golf. There are, I admit, certain drawbacks attendant on their presence on the links. I shall not readily forget the occasion on which a low, raking drive of mine at the eleventh struck the ladies' tee-box squarely and came back and stunned my caddie, causing me to lose stroke and distance. Nevertheless I hold that the advantages outnumber the drawbacks. Golf humanises women, humbles their haughty natures, tends, in short, to knock out of their systems a certain modicum of that supercili-ousness, that swank, which makes wooing such a tough proposition for the diffident male.
  'The Rough Stuff', *The Clicking of Cuthbert*, 1922

'You are a pearl among women. You stand alone. You make the rest looks like battered repaints.'
  'The Clicking of Cuthbert', *The Clicking of Cuthbert*, 1922

Golf, like measles, should be caught young, for, if postponed to riper years, the results may be serious.
  'A Mixed Threesome', *The Clicking of Cuthbert*, 1922

'In my golfing days I have driven into people, and I was always sorry later. There is something about the reproachful eye of the victim as you meet it subsequently in the bar of the clubhouse which cannot fail to jar the man of sensibility. Like a wounded oyster.'

'The Letter of the Law', *Lord Emsworth and Others*, 1937

Clarice's head appeared over the edge of the green. And at the sight of it I uttered an involuntary cry of joy, for in her left eye – the other was closed and already assuming a blackish tint – I saw the light of love.

'There's Always Golf', *Lord Emsworth and Others*, 1937

'I am not saying that love is a bad thing, only that it is an unknown quantity. I have known cases where marriage improved a man's game, and other cases where it seemed to put him right off his stroke. There seems to be no fixed rule.'

'A Woman is Only a Woman', *The Clicking of Cuthbert*, 1922

'I am not a married man myself, so have had no experience of how it feels to have one's wife whizz off silently into the unknown; but I should imagine that it must be something like taking a full swing with a brassie and missing the ball.'

'Sundered Hearts', *The Clicking of Cuthbert*, 1922

William's sister was one of those small rose-leaf girls with big blue eyes to whom good men instinctively want to give a stroke a hole and on whom bad men automatically prey.

'The Purification of Rodney Spelvin', *The Heart of a Goof*, 1926

'Mortimer, you must choose between golf and me.'

'But, darling, I went round in a hundred and one yesterday. You can't expect a fellow to give up golf when he is at the top of his game.'

'Very well. Our engagement is at an end.'

'Don't throw me over, Betty,' pleaded Mortimer, and there was that in his voice which cut me to the heart. 'You'll make me so miserable, and when I'm miserable I always slice my approach shots.'

'A Mixed Threesome', *The Clicking of Cuthbert*, 1922

'I have seen Grace Forrester watering flowers in her garden, and on these occasions her stance struck me as graceful. Once, at a picnic, I observed her killing wasps with a teaspoon, and was impressed by the freedom of the wrist-action of her back swing.'
'A Woman is Only a Woman', *The Clicking of Cuthbert*, 1922

'I never put a club into the hand of a beginner without something of the feeling of a sculptor who surveys a mass of shapeless clay. I experience the emotions of a creator. Here, I say to myself, is a semi-sentient being into whose soulless carcase I am breathing life. A moment before, he was, though technically living, a mere clod. A moment hence he will be a golfer.'
'A Mixed Threesome', *The Clicking of Cuthbert*, 1922

'I must say I think that old buffers who hold people up and won't let them through on a golf course ought to wear some sort of a label indicating that they have pretty daughters who will be arriving shortly. Still, there it is. I gave Poskitt this juicy one, as described, and from what he said to me later in the changing room I am convinced that any suggestion on my part that I become his son-in-law will not be cordially received.'
'The Letter of the Law', *Lord Emsworth and Others*, 1937

'You know how it is. If you have a broken heart, it's bound to give you a twinge now and then, and if this happens when you are starting your down swing you neglect to let the clubhead lead.'
'There's Always Golf', *Lord Emsworth and Others*, 1937

She burst into tears. I could see the poor girl was in a highly nervous condition, so I did my best to calm her by describing how I had once done the long hole in four. My friends tell me that there is no finer soporific. Presently, just as I had reached the point where I laid my approach-putt dead from a distance of fifteen feet, she became quieter. She dried her eyes, yawned once or twice, and looked at me bravely.
'A Mixed Threesome', *The Clicking of Cuthbert*, 1922

Most divorces spring from the fact that the husband is too markedly superior to his wife at golf; this leading him, when she starts criticising his relations, to say bitter and unforgivable things about her mashie-shots.
'Rodney Fails to Qualify', *The Heart of a Goof*, 1926

President's Cup day is usually looked on as a sort of Walpurgis Night, when fearful things are abroad and the prudent golfer stays at home.

'The Letter of the Law', *Lord Emsworth and Others*, 1937

The Oldest Member's eye was deep and dreamy – the eye of a man who, as the poet says, has seen Golf steadily and seen it whole.

'The Clicking of Cuthbert', *The Clicking of Cuthbert*, 1922

There is nothing sadder in this life than the spectacle of a husband and wife with practically identical handicaps drifting apart.

'The Purification of Rodney Spelvin', *The Heart of a Goof*, 1926

The Wrecking Crew were just leaving the eighteenth tee, moving up the fairway with their caddies like one of those great race-migrations of the Middle Ages.

'Chester Forgets Himself', *The Heart of a Goof*, 1926

A golfer needs a wife. It is essential that he has a sympathetic listener always handy to whom he can relate the details of the day's play.

'Up From the Depths', *Nothing Serious*, 1950

'You ask, have I asked her to marry me? I, who am not worthy to polish the blade of her niblick! I, who have not even a thirty handicap, ask a girl to marry me who was in the semi-final of last year's Ladies' Open! No, no. I may be a *vers libre* poet, but I have some sense of what is fitting.'

'The Purification of Rodney Spelvin', *The Heart of a Goof*, 1926

He played a weak and sinful spoon shot out to the right.

'There's Always Golf', *Lord Emsworth and Others*, 1937

He would never have to suffer that greatest of all spiritual agonies, the misery of the husband whose wife insists on her playing with him daily because the doctor thinks she ought to have fresh air and exercise.

'Feet of Clay', *Nothing Serious*, 1950

'You love her?'
  'Madly.'
  'And how do you find it affects your game?'
  'I've started shanking a bit.'

The Oldest Member nodded. 'I'm sorry, but not surprised Either that or missing short putts is what generally happens on these occasions. I doubt if golfers ought to fall in love. I have known it cost men ten shots in a medal round.'
'Scratch Man', *A Few Quick Ones*, 1959

The only cloud on Angus's happiness was the fact that his great love occasionally caused him to fluff a chip shot. He would be swinging and he would suddenly think of Evangeline and jerk his head towards the sky, as if asking Heaven to make him worthy of her, thus shanking. He told me he had lost several holes that way.
'Farewell to Legs', *Lord Emsworth and Others*, 1937

He had stood addressing his ball like Lot's wife just after she had been turned into a pillar of salt. Now he wriggled like an Ouled Nail dancer in the throes of colic.
'Excelsior', *Nothing Serious*, 1950

The fourth hole found him four down and one had the feeling that he was lucky not to be five.
'Excelsior', *Nothing Serious*, 1950

'Over my dead body!'
'That would be a mashie-niblick shot,' said Sidney McMurdo.
'Feet of Clay', *Nothing Serious*, 1950

The least thing upsets him on the links. He misses short putts because of the uproar of the butterflies in the adjoining meadows.
'Ordeal by Golf', *The Clicking of Cuthbert*, 1922

STAGE
— AND —
SCREEN

I took my place among the standees at the back of the concert hall. I devoted my time to studying the faces of my neighbours, hoping to detect in them some traces of ruth and pity and what is known as kind indulgence. But not a glimmer. Like all rustic standees, these were stern, implacable men, utterly incapable of taking the broad, charitable view and realising that a fellow who comes on a platform and starts reciting about Christopher Robin going hoppity-hoppity-hop (or, alternatively, saying his prayers) does not do so from sheer wantonness but because he is a helpless victim of circumstances beyond his control. I was gazing with considerable apprehension at a particularly dangerous specimen on my left, a pleasure-seeker with hair-oil on his head and those mobile lips to which the raspberry springs automatically.

The Mating Season, 1949

Musical comedy is the Irish stew of drama. Anything may be put into it, with the certainty that it will improve the general effect.

'Bill the Bloodhound', *The Man with Two Left Feet*, 1917

A certain liveliness was beginning to manifest itself up in the gallery. The raspberry was not actually present, but he seemed to hear the beating of its wings.

'The Masked Troubadour', *Lord Emsworth and Others*, 1937

For an instant Mr Schnellenhamer was conscious of a twinge of uneasiness. Like all motion picture magnates, he had about forty seven guilty secrets, many of them recorded on paper.
'The Rise of Minna Nordstrom', *Blandings Castle and Elsewhere*, 1935

He got through the song somehow and limped off amidst roars of silence from the audience.
'Extricating Young Gussie', *The Man with Two Left Feet*, 1917

Joe Lehman, the theatrical producer, was a man of the great indoors.
Barmy in Wonderland, 1952

'You can't go by what a man in my position promises. You don't really suppose, do you, that you can run a big movie studio successfully if you go about keeping your promise all the time.'
Pearls, Girls and Monty Bodkin, 1972

'I was in musical comedy. I used to sing in the chorus, till they found out where the noise was coming from. And then I went to Hollywood. You would like Hollywood, you know. Everybody does. Girdled by the everlasting hills, bathed in eternal sunshine. And if you aren't getting divorced yourself, there's always one of your friends who is, and that gives you something to chat about in the long evenings. And it isn't half such a crazy place as they make out. I know two-three people in Hollywood that are part sane.'
The Luck of the Bodkins, 1935

The best-laid plans of mice and men end up on the cutting room floor.
Pearls, Girls and Monty Bodkin, 1972

It was a poetic drama, and the audience, though loath to do anybody an injustice, was beginning to suspect that it was written in blank verse.
Jill the Reckless, 1921

She had a sort of ethereal beauty; but then every girl you see in Hollywood has either ethereal beauty or roguish gaminerie or a dark, slumbrous face that hints at hidden passion.
   'The Rise of Minna Nordstrom', *Blandings Castle and Elsewhere*, 1935

They had gone on to the opening performance at the Flaming Youth Group Centre of one of those avant-garde plays which bring the scent of boiling cabbage across the footlights and in which the little man in the bowler hat turns out to be God.
   Service with a Smile, 1962

In order to make a song a smash it is not enough for the singer to be on top of his form. The accompanist, also, must do his bit. And the primary thing a singer expects from his accompanist is that he shall play the accompaniment of the song he is singing.
   'The Masked Troubadour', *Lord Emsworth and Others*, 1937

His nose, as he gazed at Lord Ickenham, was twitching like a rabbit's, and in the eyes behind their tortoiseshell spectacles there was dawning slowly a look of incredulous horror. It was as if he had been cast for the part of Macbeth and was starting to run through the Banquo's ghost scene.
   Uncle Fred in the Springtime, 1939

'I met a fellow in the canteen who looked as if he might be a writer of additional dialogue or the man in charge of the wind machine.'
   Pearls, Girls and Monty Bodkin, 1972

Everybody liked Bill Shannon, even in Hollywood, where nobody likes anybody.
   The Old Reliable, 1951

You can't reason with hams, and twenty minutes of Corky's society seemed to have turned Augustus Fink-Nottle from a

blameless newt-fancier into as pronounced a ham as ever drank small ports in Bodegas and called people 'Laddie'.
The Mating Season, 1949

'When a studio executive charges you, look to the left but leap to the right. This baffles the simple creature.'
Barmy in Wonderland, 1952

'I want you to come to Hollywood, and I'm going to get you. And if you think you're going to prevent me, you're trying to stop Niagara with a tennis racket. . . .'
'Came the Dawn', *Meet Mr Mulliner*, 1927

The Duke of Wigan who, as so many British dukes do, was at this time passing slowly through Hollywood. . . .
'The Rise of Minna Nordstrom', *Blandings Castle and Elsewhere*, 1935

The party of the second part, hereinafter to be called the artist, shall abstain from all ice-creams, chocolate-creams, nut sundaes, fudge and all-day suckers, hereinafter to be called candy, this to be understood to comprise doughnuts, marshmallows, pies in their season, all starchy foods and twice of chicken.
Laughing Gas, 1936

You can't heave a brick in Hollywood without beaning an English elocution teacher. I am told there are English elocution teachers making good money there who haven't even got roofs to their mouths.
Laughing Gas, 1936

'If my Aunt Julia in Hollywood had confined herself to snootering directors, harrying camera-men, and chasing supervisors up trees, nothing would have been said. But there is one thing the artist soul must not do at the Colossal-Superfine, and that is swat the Main Boss with a jewelled hand over the ear-hole.'
'Ukridge and the Home From Home', *Lord Emsworth and Others*, 1937

They seem to think that just because a girl works in the chorus she must be a sort of animated champagne-vat, spending her life dancing on supper-tables with tight stockbrokers.
Summer Lightning, 1929

Agnes Flack stood about five feet ten in her stockings, and had shoulders and forearms which would have excited the envious admiration of those muscular women in the music halls, who good-naturedly allow six brothers, three sisters and a cousin by marriage to pile themselves on her collar bone while the orchestra plays a long-drawn chord and the audience hurries out to the bar.

'Those in Peril on the Tee', *Meet Mr Mulliner*, 1929

—CHILDREN—

Like so many young men, Ambrose Biffin was accustomed to regard small boys with a slightly jaundiced eye. It was his simple creed that they wanted their heads smacked. When not having their heads smacked, they should be out of the picture altogether.

'The Passing of Ambrose', *Mr Mulliner Speaking*, 1929

The boy's face closely resembled a ripe tomato with a nose stuck on it.

'The Bishop's Move', *Meet Mr Mulliner*, 1927

Like so many infants of tender years he presented to the eye the aspect of a mass murderer suffering from an ingrowing toenail.

'Leave it to Algy', *A Few Quick Ones*, 1959

Braid Bates at that time was a young plug-ugly of some nine summers, in appearance a miniature edition of his father and in soul and temperament a combination of Dead End Kid and army mule; a freckled, hard-boiled character with a sardonic eye and a mouth which, when not occupied in eating, had a cynical twist to it. He spoke little as a general thing, but when he did speak seldom failed to find a chink in the armour.

'Rodney Has a Relapse', *Nothing Serious*, 1950

She was the type of girl you see in back streets carrying a baby nearly half as large as herself and still retaining sufficient energy to lead one little brother by the hand and shout recrimination at another in the distance.

'Lord Emsworth and the Girl Friend', *Blandings Castle and Elsewhere*, 1935

Young Thos leaned across and slipped a penny in my hand, saying 'Here, my poor man' and urging me not to spend it on drink. At any other moment this coarse ribaldry would have woken the fiend that sleeps in Bertram Wooster and led to the young pot of poison receiving another clout on the head, but I had no time now for attending to Thoses.

The Mating Season, 1949

Nanny or elder sister . . . you can't ever really lose your awe of someone who used to scrub your face with a soapy flannel.

French Leave, 1956

Jane regarded him with quiet intentness.

'Does Mother's little chickabiddy want his nose pushed sideways?' she said. 'Very well, then.'

'Rodney Has a Relapse', *Nothing Serious*, 1950

At the sound of my voice Edwin's pink-rimmed eyes came swivelling round in my direction. He looked up at me like a ferret about to pass the time of day with another ferret.

Joy in the Morning, 1947

She was feeling like a mother who, in addition to having to notify him that there is no candy, has been compelled to strike a loved child on the base of the skull with a stocking full of sand.

The Old Reliable, 1951

If ever there was a woman who could be relied on to spill the beans with a firm, unerring hand, that woman was the Old Retainer. . . . 'She told me that you wore flannel next to your skin and bedsocks in winter. And,' said Ann, 'she told me that scar on your temple was not caused by a bullet, but that you had got it when you were six years old by falling against the hatstand in the hall because you forgot to scratch the soles of your new shoes.'

Big Money, 1931

Mrs Wisdom was plump and comfortable. She looked at Berry with stolid affection, like a cow inspecting a turnip. To her, he was still the infant he had been when they had first met. Her manner towards him was always that of wise Age assisting helpless Youth through a perplexing world. She omitted no word or act that might smooth the path for him and shield him against life's myriad dangers. In winter, she thrust unwanted hot water bottles into his bed. In summer, she would speak freely, not mincing her words, of flannel next to the skin and of the wisdom of cooling off slowly when the pores had been opened.

Big Money, 1931

'I will now reveal,' said Bingo, 'why I am staying in this pest-house, tutoring a kid who requires not education in the Greek and Latin languages but a swift slosh on the base of the skull with a black-jack. . . .'

'Jeeves and the Impending Doom', *Very Good, Jeeves*, 1930

. . . the kid Clementina who, instead of sticking sedulously to her studies and learning to be a good wife and mother, spent the springtime of her life filling inkpots with sherbet.

'Jeeves and the Kid Clementina', *Very Good, Jeeves*, 1930

Young Thos, poising the bucket for an instant, discharged its contents. And old Mr Anstruther received the entire consignment. In one second, without any previous training or upbringing, he had become the wettest man in Worcestershire.

'The Love that Purifies', *Very Good, Jeeves*, 1930

He was ten years old, wore a very tight Eton suit, and had the peculiarly loathsome expression which a snub nose sometimes gives to the young.

Psmith in the City, 1910

When he says his prayers at night his eyes are ostensibly closed, but all the while he is peering through his fingers and counting the house.

'Rodney Has a Relapse', *Nothing Serious*, 1950

A small boy with a face like a prune run over by a motor bus.

Galahad at Blandings, 1964

Young Thos has carroty hair and a cynical expression, and his manner is supercilious. You would think that anyone conscious of having a mother like my Aunt Agatha and knowing it could be proved against him, would be crushed and apologetic, but this is not the case. He swanks about the place as if he'd bought it, and in conversation with a cousin lacks tact and is apt to verge on the personal.

The Mating Season, 1949

A blob-faced baby.

'Sonny Boy', *Eggs, Beans and Crumpets*, 1940

Introduced to his child in the nursing home, he recoiled with a startled 'Oi!' and as the days went by the feeling that he had run up against something red-hot in no way diminished. The only thing that prevented a father's love from faltering was the fact that there was in his possession a photograph of himself at the same early age, in which he, too, looked like a homicidal fried egg.

'Sonny Boy', *Eggs, Beans and Crumpets*, 1940

The infant was looking more than ever like some mass-assassin who has been blackballed by the Devil's Island Social and Outing Club as unfit to associate with the members.

'Sonny Boy', *Eggs, Beans and Crumpets*, 1940

'Frederick won't be staying here long, will he?' Lord Emsworth asked, with a father's pathetic eagerness.

Full Moon, 1947

Every impulse urged me to give the little snurge six of the best with a bludgeon. But you can't very well slosh a child who has just lost his eyebrows. Besides, I hadn't a bludgeon.

Joy in the Morning, 1947

A spectacled child with a mouth that hung open like a letter-box.

The Luck of the Bodkins, 1935

'One of my unswerving rules in life is never to go to a film if I am informed by my spies that there is a child in it.'

Laughing Gas, 1936

Freddie's views on babies are well defined. He is prepared to cope with them singly, if all avenues of escape are blocked and there is a nurse or mother standing by to lend aid in case of sudden hiccoughs, retchings and nauseas. Under such conditions he has even been known to offer his watch to one related by ties of blood in order that the little stranger might listen to the tick-tick. But it would be paltering with the truth to say that he likes babies. They give him, he says, a sort of grey feeling. He resents their cold stare and the supercilious and up-stage way in which they dribble out of the corner of their mouths on seeing him. Eyeing them he is conscious of doubts as to whether Man can really be Nature's last word.

'Noblesse Oblige', *Young Men in Spats*, 1936

COUNTRY
—AND—
TOWN

'I'd like to settle down in this sort of place and spend the rest of my life milking cows and taking bowlfuls of soup to the deserving villagers.'
A Damsel in Distress, 1919

In most English country towns, if the public houses do not actually outnumber the inhabitants, they all do an excellent trade. It is only when they are two to one that hard times hit them and set the innkeepers blaming the Government.
Something Fresh, 1915

In Valley Fields more lawns are cultivated, more green fly squirted with whale oil solution, and more garden rollers borrowed than anywhere else south of the river Thames. Spreading trees line its thoroughfares. . . .
Company for Henry, 1967

Bottleton East was one of those primitive communities where the native sons, largely recruited from the costermongering and leaning-up-against-the-walls-of-public-houses industries, have a primitive sense of humour and think things funny that are not funny at all.
Cocktail Time, 1958

Maiden Eggesford, like so many of our rural hamlets, is not at its best and brightest on a Sunday. When you have walked down the main street and looked at the Jubilee Watering Trough, there is nothing much to do except go home and then come out again and walk down the main street once more and take another look at the Jubilee Watering Trough.
'Tried in the Furnace', *Young Men in Spats*, 1936

In places like Bottleton East, when you are having a scrap and your antagonist falls, you don't wait for anyone to count ten – you kick him in the slats. This is a local rule.
'The Masked Troubadour', *Lord Emsworth and Others*, 1937

The Emsworth Arms' idea of a writing room was an almost pitch dark cubbyhole with no paper or pens, and in the ink-pot only a curious sediment that looked like something imported from the Florida Everglades.

Pigs Have Wings, 1952

Steeple Bumpleigh was a hamlet rich in honeysuckle-covered cottages and apple-cheeked villagers, but that let it out. It had only one shop, that so ably conducted by Mrs Greenlees opposite the Jubilee Watering Trough, and this, after it had supplied you with string, pink sweets, sides of bacon, tinned goods and Old Moore's Almanac, was a spent force.

Joy in the Morning, 1947

It was a peculiarly beastly little street. Situated in the middle of one of those districts where London breaks out into a sort of eczema of red brick, it consists of two parallel rows of semi-detached villas, all exactly alike, each guarded by a ragged evergreen hedge, each with coloured glass of an extremely regrettable nature let into the panels of the front door; and sensitive young impressionists from the artists' colony up Holland Park way may sometimes be seen stumbling through it with hands over their eyes, muttering between clenched teeth 'How long? How long?'

Leave it to Psmith, 1923

Except for an occasional lecture by the vicar on his holiday in the Holy Land, illustrated by lantern slides, there was not a great deal of night-life in Dovetail Hammer.

Cocktail Time, 1958

The two-forty-five express stood at the platform with that air of well-bred reserve which is characteristic of Paddington trains. Lord Ickenham was all that was jovial and debonair. Tilting his hat at a jaunty angle, he gazed about him with approval at the decorous station which has for so many years echoed to the tread of county families.

'To one like myself,' he said, 'who, living in Hampshire, gets out of the metropolis, when he is fortunate enough to get into it, *via* Waterloo, there is something very soothing in the note of refined calm which Paddington strikes. At Waterloo, all is hustle and bustle, and the society tends to be mixed. Here a leisured peace prevails, and you get only the best people – cultured men accustomed to mingle with basset hounds and women in tailored suits who look like horses.'

Uncle Fred in the Springtime, 1939

Lord Uffenham descended the broad staircase of the Athenaeum with one hand glued to the arm of the worried-looking Bishop, with whom he was discussing Supralapsarian-ism. At the sight of Anne he relaxed his grip, and the Bishop shot gratefully off in the direction of the Silence Room.

Money in the Bank, 1946

'I daresay you know these Folk Dance people, Corky. They tie bells to their trousers and dance old rustic dances showing that it takes all sorts to make a world.'

'The Come-Back of Battling Billson', *Lord Emsworth and Others*, 1937

A messenger boy, two shabby men engaged in non-essential industries, and a shop girl paused to observe the scene. Time was not of the essence to these confirmed sight-seers. The shop girl was late already, so it didn't matter if she was any later; the messenger boy had nothing on hand except a message marked 'Important. Rush.'; and as for the two shabby men, their only immediate plans consisted of getting to some public house and leaning against the wall.

A Damsel in Distress, 1919

It was a country house dinner party. No fewer than ten of Hampshire's more prominent stiffs had been invited to the trough, and they stuck on like limpets long after any competent chucker-out would have bounced them. No doubt, if you have gone to the sweat of driving twenty miles to a house to dine, you don't feel like snatching a chop and dashing off. You hang on for the musical evening and the drinks at ten-thirty.

The Mating Season, 1949

'The last time I played in a village cricket match,' said Psmith, 'I was caught at point by a man in braces. It would have been madness to risk another such shock to my system.'

Mike, 1909

Halsey Court in Mayfair never bothered much about sunshine. What it specialised in was the smell of cooking cabbage.

Money in the Bank, 1946

In one hand he was carrying a double-barrelled gun, in the other a posy of dead rabbits . . . a portable Morgue.

'Unpleasantness at Bludleigh Court', *Mr Mulliner Speaking*, 1929

'I suppose it would be a breach of hospitality if I socked my hostess's sister in the eye?'

'The County would purse its lips.'

Spring Fever, 1948

South Kensington . . . where sin stalks naked through the dark alleys and only might is right.

Service with a Smile, 1962

'All the Wellbeloveds have been as mad as March hatters. It was his grandfather, Ezekiel Wellbeloved, who took off his trousers one snowy afternoon in the High Street and gave them to a passer-by, saying he wouldn't be needing them any longer, as the end of the world was coming that evening at five-thirty sharp.'

Pigs Have Wings, 1952

'Have you any conception of what would happen were my wife to learn that I was a millionaire? Do you think I should be allowed to go on living in Valley Fields, the place I love, and continue to be a house agent, the work I love? Do you suppose I should be allowed to keep my old friends, like Mr Wrenn of San Rafael, with whom I play chess on Saturdays, and feed rabbits in my shirt sleeves? No, I should be whisked off to a flat in Mayfair, I should have to spend long months in the south of France, a butler would be engaged and I should have to dress for dinner every night. I should have to join a London club, take a box at the opera, learn to play polo,' said Mr Cornelius, allowing his morbid fancy to run away with him a little. . . .

Ice in the Bedroom, 1961

In all properly regulated country houses the hours between tea and dinner are set aside for letter-writing. The strength of the company retire to their rooms, heavy with muffins, and settle down to a leisurely disposal of their correspondence. Those who fall asleep try again next day.

Pigs Have Wings, 1952

The village hall was one of those mid-Victorian jobs in glazed red brick which always seem to bob up in these olde-worlde hamlets and do so much to encourage the drift to the towns. Its interior, like those of all the joints of its kind I've ever come across, was dingy and fuggy and smelled in about equal proportions of apples, chalk, damp plaster, Boy Scouts and the sturdy English peasantry.

The Mating Season, 1949

The lamp-and-mop room at the station was a dark and sinister apartment, smelling strongly of oil and porters.

'The Truth about George', *Meet Mr Mulliner*, 1927

'Ever since you very decently gave me a roof over my head, I've been giving a lot of thought to life in the suburbs, and one thing that struck me was what I may call its garden fence aspect. Each house has its little garden, and each garden has its fence, and sooner or later the boy in House A is going to meet the girl in House B across it.'

Company for Henry, 1967

Market Snodsbury is mostly chapel folk with a moral code that would have struck Torquemada as too rigid.

Much Obliged, Jeeves, 1971

'I'm a Justice of the Peace. I sit on the Bench at our local Sessions and put it across the criminal classes when they start getting above themselves.'

The Mating Season, 1949

Bridmouth-on-Sea is notorious for its invigorating air. Corpses at Bridmouth-on-Sea leap from their biers and dance round the maypole.

Aunts Aren't Gentlemen, 1974

There are clubs in London where talk is as the crackling of thorns under a pot and it is *de rigueur* to throw lumps of sugar across the room at personal friends, and other, more sedate clubs where silence reigns and the inmates curl up in armchairs, close their eyes and leave the rest to Nature. Lord Uffenham's was one of the latter. In its smoking room this afternoon there were present, besides his lordship and Mortimer Bayliss, some dozen living corpses, all breathing gently with their eyes closed and letting the world go by.

Something Fishy, 1957

Bottleton East is crammed from end to end with costermongers dealing in tomatoes, potatoes, Brussels sprouts and fruits in their season, and it is a very negligent audience there that forgets to attend a place of entertainment with full pockets.

'The Masked Troubadour', *Lord Emsworth and Others*, 1937

It is fortunate that the quality of country hotel turbot is such that you do not notice much difference when it turns to ashes in your mouth, for this is what Monty's turbot was doing now.

Heavy Weather, 1933

She went out into the Park to look at rabbits. Never seen one before. Not running about, that is, with all its insides in it.

If I Were You, 1931

The club was a richly but gloomily furnished building in Pall Mall, a place of soft carpets, shaded lights, and whispers. Grave, elderly men moved noiselessly to and fro, or sat in meditative silence in deep armchairs. Sometimes the visitor felt that he was in a cathedral, sometimes in a Turkish bath; while now and then there was a suggestion of the waiting-room of a more than usually prosperous dentist.

'Ahead of Schedule', *The Man Upstairs*, 1914

You know how it is in these remote rural districts. Life tends at times to get a bit slow. There's nothing much to do in the long winter evenings but listen to the radio and brood on what a tick your neighbour is. You find yourself remembering how Farmer Giles did you down over the sale of your pig, and Farmer Giles finds himself remembering that it was your son, Ernest, who bunged the half-brick at his horse on the second Sunday before Septuagesima.

'The Ordeal of Young Tuppy', *Very Good, Jeeves*, 1930

To attract attention in the dining room of the Senior Conservative Club between the hours of one and one-thirty, you have to be a mutton chop, not an earl.

Something Fresh, 1915

Hosts at English country houses are divided into two classes: those who, when helpless guests are in their power, show them the stables, and those who show them the model dairy. There is also a sub-division which shows them the begonias.

Uncle Dynamite, 1948

Not for many a day had this street-lounger so enjoyed himself. In an arid world containing too few goes of gin and too many policemen, a world in which the poor were oppressed and could seldom even enjoy a quiet cigar without having their fingers trodden on, he found himself for the moment contented, happy and expectant. This looked like a row between toffs, and of all things that most intrigued him a row between toffs ranked highest.

A Damsel in Distress, 1919

The floor was crowded with all that was best and noblest in the county; so that a half-brick, hurled at any given moment, must infallibly have spilt blue blood.

A Damsel in Distress, 1919

About the station of Ashenden Oakshott there is little or nothing to rouse the emotions and purge the soul with pity and terror. Once you have seen the stationmaster's whiskers, which are of a Victorian bushiness and give the impression of having been grown under glass, you have drained it of all it has to offer in the way of thrills, unless you are one of those easily excited persons who can find drama in the spectacle of a small porter wrestling with a series of large milk cans. 'Placid' is the word that springs to the lips.

Uncle Dynamite, 1948

In its general essentials the coffee-room at the Goose and Gherkin differed very little from the coffee-rooms of all the other inns that nestle by the wayside in England and keep the island race from dying of thirst. It had the usual dim religious light, the customary pictures of *The Stag at Bay* and *The Huguenot's Farewell* over the mantelpieces, the same cruets and bottles of sauce and the traditional ozone-like smell of mixed pickles, gravy soup, boiled potatoes, waiters and old cheese.

Ring for Jeeves, 1953

'I always thought,' said Leila Yorke, 'the suburbs were miles of ghastly little semi-detached houses full of worn-out women ironing shirts and haggard men with coughs wondering where the rent was coming from. And now look at this joint we've fetched up in.'

Ice in the Bedroom, 1961

In Bottleton East on every side merry matrons sat calling each other names on doorsteps. Cheery cats fought among the garbage-pails. From the busy public house came the sound of mouth organ and song. While, as for the children, who were present in numerous quantities, so far from crying for bread, as he had been led to expect, they were playing hop-scotch all over the pavements. The whole atmosphere, in a word, was, he tells me, more like that of Guest Night at the National Liberal Club than anything he had ever encountered.

'Archibald and the Masses', *Young Men in Spats*, 1936

POLICE

There was a good deal of mud on the policeman's face, but not enough to hide the wounded expression.
The Code of the Woosters, 1938

'Ho!' said Police Constable Popjoy. He was a man of few words, and those mostly of one syllable.
'Big Business', *A Few Quick Ones*, 1959

From the fact that the top of his helmet moved sharply in the direction of the stars, I knew that Police Constable Stilton had drawn himself up to his full height. He found himself, however, in a somewhat embarrassing position. He could not come back with anything really snappy, Uncle Percy being a Justice of the Peace and, as such, able to put it across him like the dickens if he talked out of turn. Besides being his future father-in-law.
Joy in the Morning, 1947

Chimp Twist found himself confronting a policeman so large that his bones turned to water and his heart fluttered within him like a caged bird. He was allergic to all policemen, but the last variety he would have wished to encounter at such a moment was the large.
Ice in the Bedroom, 1961

The policeman was taut and alert, as became an officer who, after a jog-trot existence of Saturday drunks and failures to abate smoky chimneys, finds himself faced for the first time with crime on a colossal scale.
Uncle Dynamite, 1948

'Don't blame me, Pongo,' said Lord Ickenham, 'if Lady Constance takes her lorgnette to you. God bless my soul, though, you can't compare the lorgnettes of today with the ones I used to know as a boy. I remember walking one day in Grosvenor Square with my aunt Brenda and her pug dog Jabberwocky, and a policeman came up and said the latter ought to be wearing a muzzle. My aunt made no verbal reply. She merely whipped her lorgnette from its holster and looked at the man, who gave one choking gasp and fell back against the railings, without a mark on him but with an awful look of horror in his staring eyes, as if he had seen some dreadful sight. A doctor was sent for, and they managed to bring him round, but he was never the same again. He had to leave the Force, and eventually drifted into the grocery business. And that is how Sir Thomas Lipton got his start.'

Uncle Fred in the Springtime, 1939

In New York detectives' hats don't take off.

'Fate', *Young Men in Spats*, 1936

'Why, I was twice the man he is,' said Galahad. 'How many policemen do you think it used to take to shift me from the Alhambra to Vine Street when I was in my prime? Two! Sometimes three. And one walking behind carrying my hat.'

Summer Lightning, 1929

'I shall never forget you that day at the dog races. Sombre is the only word to describe your attitude as the cop's fingers closed on your coat collar.'

Uncle Dynamite, 1948

The band of the local police force were seating themselves with the grim determination of those who know that they are going to play the soldiers' chorus out of 'Faust'. The band at the School Sports had played the soldiers' chorus out of 'Faust' every year for decades past, and will in all probability play it for decades to come.

The Pothunters, 1902

A rich, deep, soft, soothing voice slid into the heated scene like the Holy Grail sliding athwart a sunbeam.

'What's all this?'

A vast policeman had materialised from nowhere.

A Damsel in Distress, 1919

Of the broad general principle of hitting the police force in the eye he had always thoroughly approved. You could not, in his opinion, do it too much or too often.

Galahad at Blandings, 1964

'I propose to blot this flatty from the London scene. Do you know what he'll rue? The day he was born, that's what he'll rue.'
Frozen Assets, 1964

'At the old Gardenia,' said Galahad, 'the bouncers used to fight for the privilege of throwing me out, and there seldom failed to be a couple of the gendarmerie waiting in the street as I shot through the door, on me like wolves and intensely sceptical of my sobriety.'
Galahad at Blandings, 1964

The menacing way in which the policeman hopped on his bicycle and pedalled off spoke louder than words. I don't think I have ever seen anyone pedal with a more sinister touch to the ankle work.
Joy in the Morning, 1947

Unlike most of his lighthearted companions of the Drones Club, who rather made pets of policemen, tipping them when in funds and stealing their helmets on Boat Race night, Pongo always had a horror of the Force.
Uncle Dynamite, 1948

On Constable Potter's face was that hard, keen look which comes into the faces of policemen when they intend to do their duty pitilessly and crush a criminal like a snake beneath the heel. It was the look which Constable Potter's face wore when he was waiting beneath a tree to apprehend a small boy who was up in its branches stealing apples, the merciless expression that turned it to flint when he called at a house to serve a summons on somebody for moving pigs without a permit.
Uncle Dynamite, 1948

'What have you been doing to inflame Police Constable Stilton, Bertie? I met him just now and asked if he had seen you, and he turned vermilion and gnashed every tooth in his head. I don't think I've ever seen a more incandescent copper.'
Joy in the Morning, 1947

Since they started that Police College at Hendon, the Force has become congested with one's old buddies. I remember Barmy Fotheringay-Phipps describing to me with gestures his emotions on being pinched in Leicester Square on Boat Race night by his younger brother George.
Joy in the Morning, 1947

The cop, who was reading the Sunday paper while he stirred his coffee absently with the muzzle of his automatic, said he saw where this new Purity Drive seemed to be gaining ground.
   Laughing Gas, 1936

There was a howl of fury which caused the local policeman, who had just been about to turn into the street, to stop and tie his bootlace.
   Summer Moonshine, 1938

Stilton Cheesewright was now a country policeman . . . a fine figure of a young fellow as far northwards as the neck, but above that solid concrete. I could not see him as a member of the Big Four. Far more likely that he would end up as one of those Scotland Yard bunglers who used, if you remember, always to be getting into Sherlock Holmes's hair.
   Joy in the Morning, 1947

FAMILY AFFAIRS

Years before, when a boy, and romantic as most boys are, his lordship had sometimes regretted that the Emsworths, though an ancient clan, did not possess a Family Curse. How little he had suspected that he was shortly to become the father of it.

'Lord Emsworth Acts for the Best', *Blandings Castle and Elsewhere*, 1935

One felt immediately on seeing Lady Constance that there stood the daughter of a hundred earls, just as when confronted with Lord Emsworth one had the impression that one had encountered the son of a hundred tramp cyclists.

A Pelican at Blandings, 1969

As he kissed his mother, Ronnie Fish was aware of something of the feeling which he had had in his boxing days when shaking hands with an unpleasant-looking opponent.

Heavy Weather, 1933

'My dear Ronald . . . that tie!'

Ronnie Fish gazed at her lingeringly. It needed, he felt, but this. Poison was running through his veins, his world was rocking, green-eyed devils were shrieking mockery in his ears, and along came blasted aunts babbling of ties. It was as if somebody had touched Othello on the arm as he poised the pillow and criticised the cut of his doublet.

Heavy Weather, 1933

'Ronnie Fish says his Aunt Constance has to be seen to be believed. Hugo Carmody paled beneath his tan when he spoke of her. Monty Bodkin strongly suspects that she conducts human sacrifices at the time of the full moon.'

'Nonsense. These boys exaggerate so. Probably a gentle, sweet-faced lady of the old school, with mittens.'

Uncle Fred in the Springtime, 1939

'She had wanted to borrow my aunt's brooch,' said Ukridge, 'but I was firm and wouldn't let her have it – partly on principle and partly because I had pawned it the day before.'
'Ukridge and the Home from Home', *Lord Emsworth and Others*, 1937

Unlike the male codfish, which, suddenly finding itself the parent of three million five hundred thousand little codfish, cheerfully resolves to love them all, the British aristocracy is apt to look with a somewhat jaundiced eye on its younger sons.
'The Custody of the Pumpkin', *Blandings Castle and Elsewhere*, 1935

There are, of course, many ways of saying 'Well!' The speaker who had the floor at the moment – Dame Daphne Winkworth – said it rather in the manner of the prudish Queen of a monarch of Babylon who has happened to wander into the banqueting hall just as the orgy is beginning to go nicely.
'Well!' she said.
Of course what Corky had told me about Esmond Haddock's aunt-fixation ought to have prepared me for it, but I must say I was shocked at his deportment at this juncture. It was the deportment of a craven and a worm. Possibly stimulated by my getting on a chair, he had climbed on to the table and was using a banana as a hunting-crop, and he now came down like an apologetic sack of coals, his whole demeanour so crushed and cringing that I could hardly bear to look at him.
The Mating Season, 1949

As always when fate had linked Pongo's movements with his uncle's he was feeling like a man floating over Niagara Falls in a barrel.
Uncle Fred in the Springtime, 1939

'I know very little of you, true, but anyone the mention of whose name can make Father swallow his lunch the wrong way cannot be wholly bad.'
Aunts Aren't Gentlemen, 1974

'The fact of the matter is, laddie, there's nothing in being an earl nowadays. It's a mug's game. If ever they try to make you one, punch them in the eye and run. And being an earl's son and heir is one degree worse.'
Big Money, 1931

He was one of those young men who must be heirs or nothing. This is the age of the specialist, and years ago Rollo – in the present unsatisfactory state of the law parents may still christen a child Rollo – had settled on his career. Even as a boy, hardly capable of connected thought, he had been convinced that his speciality, the one thing he could do really well, was to inherit money. All he wanted was a chance. It would be bitter if Fate should withhold it from him.

'Ahead of Schedule', *The Man Upstairs*, 1914

Captain Jack Fosdyke was fully occupied with trying to keep the rain from going down the back of his neck and reminding himself that Agnes was the only niece of Josiah Flack, a man who had a deep sense of family obligations, more money than you could shake a stick at, and one foot in the grave.

'Feet of Clay', *Nothing Serious*, 1950

Sir Raymond's attitude towards those about him – his nephew Cosmo, his butler Peasemarch, his partners at bridge, the waiters at the Demosthenes and, in particular, his sister, Phoebe Wisdom, who kept house for him and was reduced by him to a blob of tearful jelly almost daily – was always that of an irritable tribal god who intends to stand no nonsense from his worshippers and is prepared, should the smoked offering fall in any way short of the highest standard, to say it with thunderbolts. To have his top hat knocked off with a Brazil nut would, in Lord Ickenham's opinion, make him a better, deeper, more lovable man.

Cocktail Time, 1958

A head waiter makes good money, but he can always do with a devoted son who pays surtax.

French Leave, 1956

The shock to Colonel Wedge of finding that what he had taken for a pile of old clothes was alive and a relation by marriage caused him to speak a little sharply.

Full Moon, 1947

'I say,' he said, 'my father's missing.'

'On how many cylinders?' asked Lord Bromborough. He was a man who liked his joke of a morning.

'Buried Treasure', *Lord Emsworth and Others*, 1937

Her father may not be able any longer to whale the tar out of her with his walking stick as in the good old days, but he can cut off her pocket money and send her to stay with her grandmother in Tunbridge Wells, where she will have to look after seven cats and attend divine service three times on Sunday.

Aunts Aren't Gentlemen, 1974

'Sisters are a mistake, Clarence. You should have set your face against them from the outset.'

Pigs Have Wings, 1952

If there is one thing that pierces the armour of an English father of the upper classes, it is to be looked down on by his younger son. Little wonder that Lord Emsworth, as he toddled along the road, was gritting his teeth. A weaker man would have gnashed them.

'Birth of a Salesman', *Nothing Serious*, 1950

She was a veteran of too many fine old crusted family rows not to be able to detect a strained atmosphere when she saw one.

Heavy Weather, 1933

Lady Constance spurned the grass with a frenzied foot. She would have preferred to have kicked her brother with it, but one has one's breeding.

Heavy Weather, 1933

His niece Angela was a pretty girl, with fair hair and blue eyes which in their softer moments probably reminded all sorts of people of twin lagoons slumbering beneath a southern sky. This, however, was not one of those moments. To Lord Emsworth, as they met his, they looked like something out of an oxy-acetylene blowpipe.

'Pig-Hoo-o-o-o-ey!' *Blandings Castle and Elsewhere*, 1935

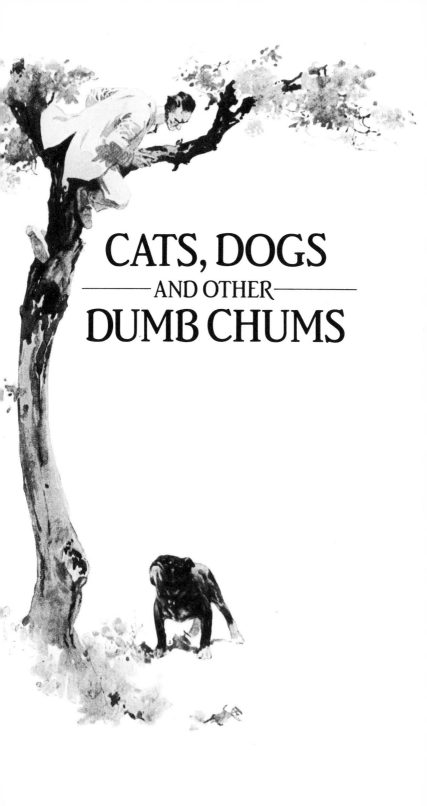

CATS, DOGS
—————AND OTHER—————
DUMB CHUMS

Any dog will tell you what these prize-ribbon dogs are like. Their heads are so swelled they have to go into their kennels backwards.

'The Mixer – Part 2', *The Man with Two Left Feet*, 1917

The world is divided into those who can stop dog-fights and those who cannot.

'Ruth in Exile', *The Man Upstairs*, 1914

[A dog working up to a fight.] To the ears of those present there came, faintly at first, a low, throaty sound, like the far-off gargling of an octogenarian with bronchial trouble.

'The Go-Getter', *Blandings Castle and Elsewhere*, 1935

Ann detached a piece of cake and dropped it before the Peke. The Peke sniffed at it disparagingly, and resumed its steady gaze. It wanted chicken. It is the simple creed of the Peke that, where two human beings are gathered together to eat, chicken must enter into the proceedings somewhere.

Big Money, 1931

The Aberdeen terrier gave me an unpleasant look and said something under his breath in Gaelic.

The Code of the Woosters, 1938

The cat had that air of portly well-being which we associate with those who dwell in cathedral closes.

'The Story of Webster', *Mulliner Nights*, 1933

The spaniels were barking. They had never seen a man sitting on a roof before and suspected a Red plot.

Summer Moonshine, 1938

'The dog is much too fat. He has just had half my breakfast. . . . I sometimes think he's a tapeworm cunningly disguised as a dachshund.'

Do Butlers Burgle Banks?, 1968

'We have no evidence whatsoever that Sir Galahad was ever called upon to do anything half as dangerous as stopping a dog-fight. And anyway, he wore armour. Give me a suit of mail, reaching well down over the ankles, and I will willingly intervene in a hundred dog-fights. But in thin flannel trousers, no!'
The Girl on the Boat, 1922

The Pekinese dog was hurling abuse in Chinese.
'Birth of a Salesman', *Nothing Serious*, 1950

This once saintly cat became a Bohemian of Bohemians. His days started early and finished late, and were a mere welter of brawling and loose gallantry.
'Cats Will be Cats', *Mulliner Nights*, 1933

The Peke followed him. It appeared to have no legs, but to move by faith alone.
'Lord Emsworth Acts for the Best', *Blandings Castle and Elsewhere*, 1935

Too often, when you introduce a ringer into a gaggle of Pekes, there ensues a scrap like New Year's Eve in Madrid: but tonight, after a certain amount of tentative sniffing, the home team issued their OK, and he left them all curled up in their baskets like so many members of the Athenaeum.
'Bingo and the Peke Crisis', *Eggs, Beans and Crumpets*, 1940

It was one of those hairy, nondescript dogs, and its gaze was cold, wary and suspicious, like that of a stockbroker who thinks someone is going to play the confidence trick on him.
'Lord Emsworth and the Girl Friend', *Blandings Castle and Elsewhere*, 1935

He was rather a sentimental man, who subscribed to homes for unwanted dogs and cats and rarely failed to cry when watching a motion picture with a sad ending.
Do Butlers Burgle Banks?, 1968

Now, just before the tiger of the jungle springs upon its prey, I am told by chaps who knows tigers of the jungle, there is always a moment when it pauses, flexing its muscles and rubbing its feet in the resin.
'The Masked Troubadour', *Lord Emsworth and Others*, 1937

'Say, Pollen, do you know anything about birds?'

'Yes, sir.'

'How are you on linnets? Do you happen to know what sort of a noise they make?'

'Yes, sir. The rough song of the linnet is "Tolic-gow-gow, tolic-joey-fair, tolic-hickey-gee, tolic-equay-quake, tuc-tuc-whizzie, tuc-tuc-joey, equay-quake-a-weet, tuc-tuc-wheet." '

Summer Moonshine, 1938

The house was a frothing maelstrom of dumb chums.

'Goodbye to All Cats', *Young Men in Spats*, 1936

It looked something like a pen-wiper and something like a piece of hearth-rug. A second and keener inspection revealed it as a Pekinese puppy.

'Goodbye to All Cats', *Young Men in Spats*, 1936

DRINKING
— AND —
HANGOVERS

You'd remember all right if you'd had a mint julep in America. Insidious things. They creep up on you like a baby sister and slide their little hands into yours and the next thing you know the Judge is telling you to pay the clerk of the court fifty dollars.
Summer Lightning, 1929

It just shows, what any member of Parliament will tell you, that if you want real oratory, the preliminary noggin is essential. Unless pie-eyed, you cannot hope to grip.
Right Ho, Jeeves, 1934

The barman recommended a 'lightning whizzer', an invention of his own. He said it was what rabbits trained on when they were matched against grizzly bears, and there was only one instance on record of the bear having lasted three rounds.
'Extricating Young Gussie', *The Man with Two Left Feet*, 1917

Whether from some hereditary taint, or because he promised his mother he wouldn't, or simply because he does not like the taste of the stuff, Gussie Fink-Nottle has never in the whole course of his career pushed so much as the simplest gin-and-tonic over the larynx.
Right Ho, Jeeves, 1934

As sober as a teetotal Girl Guide.
Thank You, Jeeves, 1934

Tanked to the uvula.
Frozen Assets, 1964

Climbing into the bed as it came round the second time . . .
'The Story of William', *Meet Mr Mulliner*, 1927

Tipton shook his head, and uttered a sharp howl. There are times when shaking the head creates an illusion that one has

met Jael, the wife of Heber, incurred her displeasure and started her going into her celebrated routine.
Galahad at Blandings, 1965

He was in the frame of mind when he would have liked to meet Joe Louis and pick a quarrel with him.
Uncle Dynamite, 1948

The effect was instantaneous and gratifying. As he drained his first glass, it seemed to him that a torchlight procession, of whose existence he had hitherto not been aware, had begun to march down his throat and explore the recesses of his stomach. The second glass, though slightly too heavily charged with molten lava, was extremely palatable. It helped the torchlight procession along by adding to it a brass band of singular sweetness of tone. And with the third somebody began to touch off fireworks in his head.
'The Story of William', *Meet Mr Mulliner*, 1927

He woke next morning on the floor of his bedroom and shot up to the ceiling when a sparrow on the windowsill chirped unexpectedly.
'The Right Approach', *A Few Quick Ones*, 1959

With the possible exception of Mrs Emily Post, a few of the haughtier Duchesses and the late Cornelia mother of the Gracchi, the British barmaid, trained from earliest years to behave with queenly dignity under the most testing conditions, stands alone in the matter of poise. . . . In her professional capacity Maudie Montrose had seen far too many members of the Peerage thrown out of the bar over which she presided for blue blood to mean anything to her.
Pigs Have Wings, 1952

A young man with dark circles under his eyes was propping himself up against a penny-in-the-slot machine. An undertaker, passing at that moment, would have looked at this young man sharply, scenting business. So would a buzzard.
The Luck of the Bodkins, 1935

She made me feel there was nothing I wouldn't do for her. She was rather like one of those innocent-tasting American drinks which creep imperceptibly into your system so that, before you know what you're doing, you're starting out to reform the world, by force if necessary, and pausing on your way to tell a large man in the corner that, if he looks at you like that, you will knock his head off.

'The Artistic Career of Corky', *Carry on, Jeeves*, 1925

What was actually in the champagne supplied to Barolini and purveyed by him to the public, such as were reckless enough to drink it, at eight shillings a bottle remains a secret between its maker and his Maker.

'Ukridge's Accident Syndicate', *Ukridge*, 1924

Galahad had discovered the prime grand secret of eternal youth – to keep the decanter circulating and never to go to bed before four in the morning.

Full Moon, 1947

After the second glass of champagne his mental outlook underwent a change. Where before he had been a mere toad beneath the harrow, he had been converted into an up-and-coming toad which seethed with rebellion.

Pearls, Girls and Monty Bodkin, 1972

He tottered blindly towards the bar like a camel making for an oasis after a hard day at the office.

'Life with Freddie', *Plum Pie*, 1966

'It has frequently happened,' said Ukridge, 'that a good go at the port at a critical moment has made all the difference to me as a thinking force. The stuff seems to act directly on the little grey cells, causing them to flex their muscles and chuck their chests out. A stiff whisky and soda sometimes has a similar effect, I have noticed, but port never fails.'

'Success Story', *Nothing Serious*, 1950

'The way you waded into that port was like a camel arriving at an oasis after a long journey through desert sands. It was as if you had received private word from Jimmy that he wanted his cellar emptied quick so that he could turn it into a games room.'

Aunts Aren't Gentlemen, 1974

Statisticians, who have gone carefully into the figures – the name of Schwertfeger of Berlin is one that springs to the mind – inform us that of young men who have just received a negative answer to a proposal of marriage (and with these must, of course, be grouped those whose engagements have been broken off) 6.08% clench their hands and stare silently before them,

12.02% take the next train to the Rocky Mountains and shoot grizzlies while 11.07% sit down at their desks and become modern novelists. The first impulse of the remainder – and these, it will be seen, constitute a large majority – is to nip off round the corner and get a good, stiff drink. Into this class Packy fell.

Hot Water, 1932

The foundation of the beverage manufactured by Mr Silvers seemed to be neat vitriol, but, once you had got used to the top of your head going up and down like the lid of a kettle with boiling water in it, the effects were far from unpleasant. Mr Silvers may not have had ideals, but he unquestionably knew what to do when you handed him a still and a potato.

'Fate', *Young Men in Spats*, 1936

Mr Gedge was not at the peak of his form. He was conscious of a dark sepia taste in his mouth and a general disinclination for any kind of thought or action. Outside the birds were singing merrily and he wished they wouldn't.

Hot Water, 1932

I always say that if you've seen one Gentleman of the Press having delirium tremens, you've seen them all.

Bachelors Anonymous, 1973

Bookmakers had called him by his pet name, barmaids had simpered beneath his gallant chaff. He had heard the chimes at midnight. And when he had looked in at the Old Gardenia, commissionaires had fought for the privilege of throwing him out. A man, in a word, who should never have been taught to write and who, if unhappily gifted with that ability, should have been restrained by Act of Parliament from writing reminiscences.

Summer Lightning, 1929

The thirst of which he was dying was one of those lively young thirsts which seem to start at the soles of the feet and get worse all the way up.

Uncle Dynamite, 1948

Gussie got lit up like a candelabra and in that condition presented the prizes.

The Mating Season, 1949

Freddie nipped round the corner to the all-night chemist's and returned with a magic bottle guaranteed to relieve an ostrich after a surfeit of tenpenny nails.

Jill the Reckless, 1921

He died of cirrhosis of the liver. It costs money to die of cirrhosis of the liver.

'Success Story', *Nothing Serious*, 1950

He was in the sort of overwrought state when a fly treading a little too heavily on the carpet is enough to make a man think he's one of the extras in *All Quiet On The Western Front*.

'The Luck of the Stiffhams', *Young Men in Spats*, 1936

'Nice day,' said Marlene as she filled the order, for she was a capital conversationalist. A barmaid has to be quick as lightning with these good things.

Galahad at Blandings, 1964

SCHOOLS
— AND —
SCHOOLBOYS

There would have been serious trouble between David and Jonathan if either had persisted in dropping catches off the other's bowling.
  Mike, 1909

'Are you the Bully, the Pride of the School, or the Boy who is Led Astray and Takes to Drink in Chapter Sixteen?'
  Mike, 1909

Headmasters of private schools are divided into two classes: the workers and the runners-up-to-London.
  The Little Nugget, 1913

'There was many a sensitive lad at school who wished Lionel Green was being educated privately.'
  Money in the Bank, 1946

It is the custom nowadays to disparage the educational methods of the English public school and to maintain that they are not practical and of a kind to fit the growing boy for the problems of after-life. But you do learn one thing at a public-school, and that is how to act when somebody starts snoring. You jolly well grab a cake of soap and pop in and stuff it down the blighter's throat.
  'The Reverent Wooing of Archibald', *Mr Mulliner Speaking*, 1929

Young Thos makes rather a speciality of running away from school. He's done it twice before, once to attend a cup final and once to go hunting treasure in the Caribees, and I don't remember Aunt Agatha on either occasion as the stricken mother. Thos was the one who got stricken. Six of the best on the old spot.
  The Mating Season, 1949

The sweetest triumph of an assistant master's life is the spectacle of one boy smacking another boy's head because the latter persists in making a noise after the master has told him to stop.

The Little Nugget, 1913

From the fact that he spoke as if he had a hot potato in his mouth without getting the raspberry from the lads in the ringside seats I deduced that he must be the headmaster.

Right Ho, Jeeves, 1934

Sanstead House Preparatory School was faintly scented with a composite aroma consisting of roast beef, ink, chalk, and that curious classroom smell which is like nothing else on earth.

The Little Nugget, 1913

At the top table, on either side of the President, were seated some twenty of the elect; and it now flashed upon him that at least eight must certainly be intending to make speeches. And right in the middle of them, with a nasty, vicious look in his eye, sat a Bishop.

Anybody who has ever attended Old Boys' dinners knows that Bishops are tough stuff. They take their time, these prelates. They mouth their words and shape their periods. They roam with frightful deliberation from the grave to the gay, from the manly straightforward to the whimsically jocular. Not one of them but is good for at least twenty-five minutes.

Big Money, 1931

Augustus Beckford had two claims to popular fame. He could hold his breath longer than any other boy in the school, and he always got hold of any piece of gossip first.

The Little Nugget, 1913

George Tupper was head of the school in my last year, and he has fulfilled exactly the impeccable promise of those early days. He is in the Foreign Office, doing well and much respected. He has an earnest, pulpy heart and takes other people's troubles very seriously.

'Ukridge's Dog College', *Ukridge*, 1924

In stories of the 'Not Really a Duffer' type, where the nervous new boy, who has been found crying in the boot-room over the photograph of his sister, contrives to get an innings in a game, nobody suspects that he is really a prodigy till he hits the Bully's first ball out of the ground for six.

Mike, 1909

'You don't know anything about anything,' Mr Pynsent pointed out gently. 'It's the effect of your English public school education.'

Sam the Sudden, 1925

Every small boy rises from his bed of a morning charged with a definite quantity of devilry; and this, if he is to sleep the sound sleep of health, he has got to work off somehow before bedtime. That is why the summer term is the one a master longs for, when the interval between classes can be spent in the open. There is no pleasanter sight for a master at a private school than that of a number of boys expending their venom harmlessly in the sunshine.

The Little Nugget, 1913

The most deadly error mortal man can make, with the exception of calling a school a college, is to call a college a school.

The Pothunters, 1902

In boxing, the right cross-counter is distinctly one of those things it is more blessed to give than to receive.

The Pothunters, 1902

Veronica was radiant. Not even in the photograph taken after the Pageant in Aid of Distressed Public School Men and showing her as the Spirit of the Playing Fields of Eton had she exhibited a more boneheaded loveliness.

Full Moon, 1947

The Rev. Aubrey was taking the senior class in Bible History, and when a headmaster gets his teeth into a senior class, he does not readily sheathe the sword.

'Bramley is So Bracing', *Nothing Serious*, 1950

Burgess and Maclaine, the opposing school captains, were old acquaintances.

Mike, 1909

At Sedleigh, Psmith's attitude towards archaeological research struck a new note in the history of that neglected science. He was amiable, but patronising. He patronised fossils and he patronised ruins. If he had been confronted with the Great Pyramid, he would have patronised that.

Mike, 1909

'The last man I met who was at school with me, though some years my junior, had a long white beard and no teeth. It blurred the picture I had formed of myself as a sprightly young fellow on the threshold of life.'

Uncle Fred in the Springtime, 1939

A frightful little weed who sings alto in the choir and for the privilege of kicking whose trouser-seat the better element fight like wolves.

Laughing Gas, 1936

'Didn't Frankenstein get married?'

'Did he?' said Eggy. 'I don't know. I never met him. Harrow man, I expect.'

Laughing Gas, 1936

INSULTS
─── AND OTHER ───
HINTS OF
DISAPPROVAL

'Forget that I called you a dish-faced moron.'
'You didn't.'
'Well I meant to.'
  Spring Fever, 1948

Chimp Twist was crooked as a pretzel.
  Ice in the Bedroom, 1961

We shall soon be having Christmas at our throats.
  'Jeeves and the Greasy Bird', *Plum Pie*, 1966

She has about as much brain as a retarded billiard ball.
  Galahad at Blandings, 1964

An accordion, or stomach Steinway.
  'A Good Cigar is a Smoke', *Plum Pie*, 1966

He had just about enough intelligence to open his mouth when
he wanted to eat, but certainly no more.
  Full Moon, 1947

The cat Percy, for all his sleek exterior, was mean and bitter. He
had no music in his soul, and was fit for treasons, strategies and
spoils. One could picture him stealing milk from a sick tabby.
  'Cats Will be Cats', *Mulliner Nights*, 1933

Even at the Drones Club, where the average of intellect is not
high, it was often said of Archibald that, had his brain been
constructed of silk, he would have been hard put to it to find
sufficient material to make a canary a pair of cami-knickers.
  'The Reverent Wooing of Archibald', *Mr Mulliner Speaking*,
  1929

'Do you know what Biff would do to you, Percy Pilbeam? He'd
butter you over the pavement. You wouldn't want your block
knocked off, would you, Perce? You wouldn't want to wake up

in hospital with nurses soothing your pillow and doctors asking where you want the body sent?'
Frozen Assets, 1964

'Probably a frightful bounder who drops his aitches and has cocoa and bloaters for supper.'
Service with a Smile, 1962

She gave me the sort of look she would have given a leper she wasn't fond of.
Ice in the Bedroom, 1961

Mavis had inherited from her father that austere Puritanism which makes the old boy so avoided by the County.
'Bramley is So Bracing', *Nothing Serious*, 1950

'It's not that I don't trust you, Dunstable, it's simply that I don't trust you.'
Service with a Smile, 1962

The Duke of Dunstable had one-way pockets. He would walk ten miles in the snow to chisel a starving orphan out of tuppence.
Service with a Smile, 1962

The Duke's was the largest trouser-seat in the peerage.
Service with a Smile, 1962

'I don't want to hurt your feelings, but you must have a soul like a stevedore's undervest.'
The Old Reliable, 1951

'All I said was "I know you started to learn to play bridge this morning, Reggie, but what time this morning?", but he didn't like it.'
Do Butlers Burgle Banks?, 1968

'We now come to the Duke of Dunstable, and this is where we really shudder. His presence at it would lower the tone of a Silver Ring bookies' social and outing picnic.'
A Pelican at Blandings, 1969

'No need for you to join the Foreign Legion, where men go to forget, Clarence. You can do it comfortably without stirring a step from Blandings Castle.'
A Pelican at Blandings, 1969

'If I saw him perishing with thirst, I wouldn't give him the dew off a Brussels-sprout. And if I heard that he had been run over by a motor omnibus, I would go about trilling like a nightingale.'
A Pelican at Blandings, 1969

'I give Soapy two years,' Chimp said. 'At the end of then his head will look like a new-born billiard ball.'
Pearls, Girls and Monty Bodkin, 1972

'Your standing with father is roughly what that of Public Enemy Number One would be at the annual Policemen's Ball.'
Aunts Aren't Gentlemen, 1974

Sir Roderick sort of just waggled an eyebrow in my direction and I saw that it was back to the basket for Bertram. I never met a man who had such a knack of making a fellow feel like a waste product.
'The Rummy Affair of Old Biffy', *Carry On, Jeeves*, 1925

Chimp would have preferred not to see Dolly at all, but if he had to see her, he would have liked to do so when she had toothache or had recently been run over by a truck.
Money in the Bank, 1946

'If ever there was a pot-bellied little human louse who needed to have the stuffing knocked out of him and his remains jumped on by strong men in hobnailed boots, it is you, Mr Pott. The next time I see a mob in the street setting on you, I shall offer to hold their coats and stand by and cheer.'
Uncle Fred in the Springtime, 1939

'He says my moustache is like the faint discoloured smear left by a squashed black-beetle on the side of a kitchen sink.'
The Code of the Woosters, 1938

He's one of those men whose legs you have to count to make sure they aren't mules.
Quick Service, 1940

He spoke very highly of himself.
Uncle Fred in the Springtime, 1939

'I think you're a pig,' she said.
'A pig, maybe, but a shrewd, level-headed pig.'
The Code of the Woosters, 1938

Percy Pilbeam was a singularly uninviting young man. His eyes were too small and too close together and he marcelled his hair in a manner distressing to right-thinking people, besides having side whiskers and a small and revolting moustache. He looked to Jerry like something unpleasant out of an early Evelyn Waugh novel.
Frozen Assets, 1963

'Odd stuff, this,' said Kay, sipping her cognac. 'Probably used for taking stains out of serge suits.'
Frozen Assets, 1964

'Ickenham, you are a cad.'
'Now you're just trying to be nice. I bet you say that to all the boys.'
Service with a Smile, 1962

Our views on each other, Spode's and mine, were definite. His was that what England needed if it was to become a land fit for heroes to live in was fewer and better Woosters, while I had always felt that there was nothing wrong with England that a ton of bricks falling from a height on Spode's head wouldn't cure.
Much Obliged, Jeeves, 1971

'Come on now, young B. Wickham, smack into it,' I said, and I took a piece of cake in a marked manner. The austerity of my tone seemed to touch a nerve and kindle the fire that always slept in this vermilion-headed menace to the common weal, for

she frowned a displeased frown and told me for heaven's sake to stop goggling like a dead halibut.
Jeeves in the Offing, 1960

His was not a high code of ethics . . . indeed, in the course of a chequered career he had frequently been guilty of actions which would have caused a three-card-trick man to purse his lips and shake his head.
French Leave, 1956

Oofy, despite his colossal wealth, had always been a man who would walk ten miles in tight shoes to pick up even the meanest sum that was lying around loose.
'The Shadow Passes', *Nothing Serious*, 1950

'As a sleuth you are poor. You couldn't detect a bass drum in a telephone booth.'
'Bill the Bloodhound', *The Man with Two Left Feet*, 1917

The magistrate looked like an owl with a dash of weasel blood in him.
'The Knightly Quest of Mervyn', *Mulliner Nights*, 1933

'You poor cake-eater!' Dolly cried. 'You talk as if it needed a college education to lean a stuffed eelskin on a guy's head. . . . You simply bust him one, see? A fellow with one arm and no legs could do it.'
Sam the Sudden, 1925

As ugly a devil as you would wish to see outside the House of Commons.
Money for Nothing, 1928

He stroked his moustache fondly. It and money were the only things he loved.
Sam the Sudden, 1925

'Chimpie,' said Mr Molloy, 'I wouldn't trust you as far as a snail could make in three jumps. I wouldn't believe you not even if I knew you were speaking the truth.'
Money for Nothing, 1928

'You poor sap . . . if you had another brain, you'd just have one!'
Money for Nothing, 1928

'What was that thing you were cutting out of the paper just now, Beach?' said Hugo.

'A photograph of Mr Galahad, sir. I keep an album in which I paste items of interest relating to the Family.'

'What that album needs is an eye-witness's description of Lady Constance Keeble falling out of a window and breaking her neck.'

Summer Lightning, 1929

'If and when I find him I shall soak him so hard it'll jar his grandchildren.'

The Small Bachelor, 1927

'Alf Todd,' said Ukridge, 'has about as much chance of winning the heavy-weight championship, as a one-armed blind man in a dark room trying to shove a pound of melted butter into a wild-cat's left ear with a red-hot needle.'

'The Return of Battling Billson', *Ukridge*, 1924

'There's another thing about you that I don't like. I've forgotten what it is at the moment, but it'll come back to me soon.'

Money for Nothing, 1928

'The kind of safe this dame would have in her house would be one of the ones you borrow a hairpin to open. Or, if nobody's got a hairpin, just eat some garlic and breathe on the lock.'

Hot Water, 1932

Never again, he told himself, would he trust Confidence Trick men. They weren't honest.

Hot Water, 1932

'He is very sore at you. He says if you're drowning he'll throw you a flat-iron, but outside of that he doesn't want anything to do with you.'

Hot Water, 1932

'I've always treated this man with unremitting kindness, and if he won't do a little thing like this for me, I'll kick his spine up through his hat.'

Hot Water, 1932

'Clarence, you're an idiot!'

Even the presence of the chauffeur, Voules, could not prevent Lady Constance from saying that. After all, she was revealing no secrets. Voules had been in service at the castle quite long enough to have formed the same impression for himself.
Summer Lightning, 1929

He galloped down the stairs and lumbered into his car in what for a man of his build was practically tantamount to a trice.
Heavy Weather, 1933

She wrinkles her nose at me as if I were a drain that had got out of order.
Right Ho, Jeeves, 1934

'Have you ever tasted such filthy coffee?'

'Never,' said Joe, though he had lived in French hotels.
Summer Moonshine, 1938

He was sailing for America to add one more to the long roll of English lecturers who have done so much to keep the depression going in that unfortunate country.
Summer Moonshine, 1938

Moths had nested in his pocket book for years and raised large families.
'The Masked Troubadour', *Lord Emsworth and Others*, 1937

'Go into the silence, Butterwick. I am not speaking to you. I wouldn't speak to you if your shirt was on fire.'
Pearls, Girls and Monty Bodkin, 1972

Mr Butterwick had left his hat with the hat-check girl, but if it had been on his head, Monty would have accused him of talking through it.
Pearls, Girls and Monty Bodkin, 1972

He's got about as much intelligence as a Cabinet minister.
Much Obliged, Jeeves, 1971

'Spode's one of those silver-tongued orators you read about. Extraordinary gift of the gab he has. He could get into Parliament without straining a sinew.'

'Then why doesn't he?'

'He's a lord.'

'Don't they allow lords in?'

'No, they don't.'

'I see,' I said, rather impressed by this proof that the House of Commons drew the line somewhere.

Much Obliged, Jeeves, 1971

IMAGES

A false beard and spectacles shielded his identity from the public eye. If you had asked him, he would have said he was a Scotch business man. As a matter of fact, he looked far more like a motor-car coming through a haystack.

'Bill the Bloodhound', *The Man with Two Left Feet*, 1917

He writhed like an electric fan.

'The Aunt and the Sluggard', *Carry On, Jeeves*, 1925

There was something sort of bleak about her tone, rather as if she had swallowed an east wind.

'Jeeves and the Unbidden Guest', *Carry On, Jeeves*, 1925

Honoria Glossop is one of those robust, dynamic girls with the muscles of a welter-weight and a laugh like a squadron of cavalry charging over a tin bridge.

'The Rummy Affair of Old Biffy', *Carry On, Jeeves*, 1925

. . . an extraordinarily hefty crash. Try to imagine the Albert Hall falling on the Crystal Palace, and you will have got the rough idea.

'Jeeves and the Kid Clementina', *Very Good, Jeeves*, 1930

It was one of those still evenings you get in the summer, when you can hear a snail clear its throat a mile away.

'Jeeves Takes Charge', *Carry On, Jeeves*, 1925

I found Rocky standing beside me, with a sort of mixed expression of wistfulness and apoplexy on his face.

'The Aunt and the Sluggard', *Carry On, Jeeves*, 1925

He was turning on the charm as if through the nozzle of a hose-pipe, and it was going all over her and she liked it.

'Feet of Clay', *Nothing Serious*, 1950

He felt like a man who, chasing rainbows, has had one of them suddenly turn and bite him in the leg.
    'Anselm Gets His Chance', *Eggs, Beans and Crumpets*, 1940

Bingo sank back in his chair feeling as if he had been slapped in the eye with a wet sock.
    'The Shadow Passes', *Nothing Serious*, 1950

Old Lord Bodsham was looking like a codfish with something on its mind.
    'Bramley is So Bracing', *Nothing Serious*, 1950

He sat motionless, his soul seething within him like a welsh rabbit at the height of its fever.
    'Tangled Hearts', *Nothing Serious*, 1950

Bingo was Mr Purkiss's right-hand man. But there were many reasons that Mr Purkiss gave for his refusal to increase his salary. He placed these one by one before his right-hand man, and an hour or so later, his daily task completed, the right-hand man went on his way, feeling like a left-hand man.
    'Bingo Bans the Bomb', *Plum Pie*, 1966

He was a man with the manner suggestive of a funeral mute suffering from suppressed jaundice.
    The Little Nugget, 1913

Being in the same room as Mrs Milsom always made him feel like a murderer with particularly large feet.
    'Archibald's Benefit', *The Man Upstairs*, 1914

He was sitting at his desk with the glazed stare of one who has been struck in the thorax by a thunderbolt.
    Psmith in the City, 1910

A melancholy-looking man, he had the appearance of one who has searched for the leak in life's gas-pipe with a lighted candle.
    'The Man Who Disliked Cats', *The Man Upstairs*, 1914

He looked much more like a parrot than most parrots do. It gave strangers a momentary shock of surprise when they saw Bream Mortimer in restaurants, eating roast beef. They had the feeling that he would have preferred sunflower seeds.
    The Girl on the Boat, 1922

She gave a sniff that sounded like a nor'easter ripping the sails of a stricken vessel.

'Bramley is So Bracing', *Nothing Serious*, 1950

They moved slowly off with bowed heads, like a couple of pallbearers who have forgotten their coffin and had to go back for it.

The Mating Season, 1949

The fête was the high spot of Ashenden Oakshott's social year, when all that was bravest and fairest in the village assembled in the Manor grounds and made various kinds of whoopee. Races were run, country dances danced, bonny babies judged in order of merit in the big tent and tea and buns consumed in almost incredible quantities. Picture a blend of the Derby and a garden party at Buckingham Palace, and Belshazzar's Feast, and you have the Ashenden Oakshott Fête.

Uncle Dynamite, 1948

Angus McAllister stood glowering. His attitude was that of one sorely perplexed. So might the early bird have looked if the worm ear-marked for its breakfast had suddenly turned and snapped at it.

'Lord Emsworth and the Girl Friend', *Blandings Castle and Elsewhere*, 1935

A sort of writhing movement behind the moustache showed that Sir Aylmer was smiling, and in another moment who knows what beautiful friendship might not have begun to blossom. Unfortunately, however, before the burgeoning process could set in, Sir Aylmer's eye fell on the remains of the what-not and the smile vanished from his face like breath off a razor-blade, to be replaced by a scowl of such malignity that Pongo had the illusion that his interior organs were being scooped out with a spade or trowel.

Uncle Dynamite, 1948

Augustus Robb, except for an occasional soft hiccough, might have been a statue of himself, erected by a few friends and admirers.

Spring Fever, 1948

With 'Catsmeat' Pirbright's sister Corky the general effect is of an angel who eats lots of yeast.

The Mating Season, 1949

'You look like Helen of Troy after a good facial.'
Uncle Dynamite, 1948

He advanced towards us on leaden feet, giving the impression of having had his insides removed by a taxidermist who had forgotten to complete the operation by stuffing him.
'Joy Bells for Walter', *A Few Quick Ones*, 1959

A fruity voice, like old tawny port made audible, said 'Come in'.
Something Fresh, 1915

A small china figure represented a warrior of pre-khaki days advancing with a spear upon some adversary who, judging from the contented expression on the warrior's face, was smaller than himself.
'A Shock for Mr Brewster', *Indiscretions of Archie*, 1921

He was like one who, having survived an earthquake, is hit by an automobile.
The Little Nugget, 1913

'Here's a picture of me looking like a Zulu chieftainess taken in a coal cellar in a bad fog.'
Jill the Reckless, 1921

Conversation on the New York Subway is impossible. The ingenious gentlemen who constructed it started with the object of making it noisy. Not ordinarily noisy like a ton of coal falling onto a sheet of tin, but really noisy. So they fashioned the pillars of thin steel, and the sleepers of thin wood, and loosened all nuts, and now a Subway train in motion suggests a prolonged dynamite explosion blended with the voice of some great cataract.
Psmith, Journalist, 1915

Silent, gaping youths, at whom lunacy commissioners looked sharply and suspiciously when they met.
'A Sea of Troubles', *The Man with Two Left Feet*, 1917

He looked something between a youngish centenarian and a nonagenarian who had seen a good deal of trouble.
'Bill the Bloodhound', *The Man with Two Left Feet*, 1917

'Gussie was looking so like a halibut that if he hadn't been wearing horn-rimmed spectacles, a thing halibuts seldom do, I

might have supposed myself to be gazing on something a.w.o.l. from a fishmonger's slab.'
Stiff Upper Lip, Jeeves, 1963

He blinked, like some knight of King Arthur's court, who, galloping to perform a deed of derring-do, has had the misfortune to collide with a tree.
Uncle Dynamite, 1948

I had come, through the years, to know Gussie as a newt-fancier, a lover and a fathead, but I had never suspected him of possessing qualities as a sprinter on the flat. He was coming along like a jack-rabbit on the western prairies. I liked his ankle work.
The Mating Season, 1949

Lady Bostock made that clicking noise, like a wet finger touching a hot iron, which women use as a substitute for the masculine 'Well, I'll be damned!'.
Uncle Dynamite, 1948

For perhaps half a minute he felt so boneless that he could not have squeezed a grape.
'All's Well with Bingo', *Eggs, Beans and Crumpets*, 1940

'Mustard' Pott looks just what he is – a retired Silver Ring bookie who has been doing himself too well on the starchy foods.
Uncle Fred in the Springtime, 1939

He now retreated to the wall and seemed, as far as I could gather, to be trying to go through it. Foiled in this endeavour, he stood looking as if he had been stuffed by a good taxidermist.
The Code of the Woosters, 1938

The Duke's moustache was rising and falling like seaweed on an ebb tide.
Uncle Fred in the Springtime, 1939

Nature, stretching Horace Davenport out, had forgotten to stretch him sideways, and one could have pictured Euclid, had they met, nudging a friend and saying 'Don't look now, but this chap coming along illustrates what I was telling you about a straight line having length without breadth.'
Uncle Fred in the Springtime, 1939

I gazed at him hopefully, like a seal awaiting a bit of fish.
The Code of the Woosters, 1938

They tottered out shaking in every limb and groping their way
blindly, like guests coming away from a Lord Mayor's Banquet.
Quick Service, 1940

She is the sort of woman who makes you feel that, no matter how
suave her manner for the nonce, she is at heart a twenty-minute
egg and may start functioning at any moment.
Uncle Fred in the Springtime, 1939

Stiffy Byng is one of those girls who enjoy in equal quantities the
gall of an army mule and the calm *insouciance* of a fish on a slab of ice.
The Code of the Woosters, 1938

She was the sort of girl Pongo could see himself kissing gently on
the forehead and then going out into the sunset. He reminded
himself of Cyrano de Bergerac.
Uncle Fred in the Springtime, 1939

He was staring incredulously, like one bitten by a rabbit.
The Code of the Woosters, 1938

The door opened and Gussie's head emerged cautiously, like
that of a snail taking a look round after a thunderstorm.
The Code of the Woosters, 1938

A sniff like the tearing of a piece of calico.
The Code of the Woosters, 1938

A strange frozen sensation had come over me, rendering the
physical and mental processes below par. It was as though both
limbs and bean had been placed in a refrigerator and over-
looked for several days.
The Code of the Woosters, 1938

There had come into 'Mustard' Pott's eyes a dull glow like the
phosphorescent gleam on the stomach of a dead fish.
Uncle Fred in the Springtime, 1939

The thought curdled the blood and made me feel a dry, fluttering feeling in the pit of the stomach, as if I had swallowed a
heaping tablespoonful of butterflies.
Joy in the Morning, 1947

Mr Pott disappeared feet foremost, like a used gladiator being cleared away from the arena.
Uncle Fred in the Springtime, 1939

He crouched in the wardrobe like a weevil nestling in a biscuit.
Money in the Bank, 1946

She was staring at her plate with a sort of queenly disgust, like Mrs Siddons inspecting a caterpillar in her salad.
Quick Service, 1940

His whole aspect was that of a man who has been unexpectedly struck by lightning.
'The Editor Regrets', *Eggs, Beans and Crumpets*, 1940

As slippery as an eel dipped in butter.
Money in the Bank, 1946

Kelly was on the buxom side. In her middle forties she still retained much of the spectacular beauty of her youth, but a carelessness these last years in the matter of counting the calories had robbed her figure of its old streamlined look. Today she resembled a Ziegfeld Follies girl who had been left out in the rain and had swollen a little.
Company for Henry, 1967

He gazed at the girl like an ostrich goggling at a brass door-knob.
Uncle Fred in the Springtime, 1939

Elation and triumph in her handsome eyes, she was looking like a Roman Matron who has unexpectedly backed the winning chariot at the Circus Maximus.
Quick Service, 1940

There was a crackling sound, like a forest fire, as Mr Steptoe champed his toast. This gorilla-jawed man could get a certain amount of noise response even out of mashed potatoes, but it was when eating toast that you caught him at his best.
Quick Service, 1940

'Mustard' Pott pulled out his pack of cards and fingered it lovingly, like some grand old warrior testing the keenness of his blade before a battle.
Uncle Fred in the Springtime, 1939

Lady Hermione was looking like a cook about to give notice on the evening of the big dinner party.
Full Moon, 1947

Dame Daphne was a rugged light-heavyweight with a touch of Wallace Beery in her make-up.
The Mating Season, 1949

As he reached the end of the carpet and was about to turn about and pace back again, he stopped abruptly with one foot in the air, looking so like *The Soul's Awakening* that a seasoned art critic would have been deceived.
Uncle Dynamite, 1948

He went to the kitchen. I peered in, and there was the cook shovelling cold steak and kidney pie into him like a stevedore loading a grain ship.
Stiff Upper Lip, Jeeves, 1963

Gloria's dark beauty made her look like a serpent of old Nile. A nervous host, encountering her on her way to dine, might have been excused for wondering whether to offer her a dry martini or an asp.
Pigs Have Wings, 1952

'Parsloe was so crooked he sliced bread with a corkscrew. You watch that pig of yours like a hawk, Clarence, or before you know where you are, this fiend in human shape will be slipping pineapple bombs in her bran mash.'
Pigs Have Wings, 1952

I remained motionless, like a ventriloquist's dummy whose ventriloquist has gone off to the local and left it sitting.
Stiff Upper Lip, Jeeves, 1963

Johnny had found Lady Constance frosty. It was as though he had been for an extended period shut up in a frigidaire with Queen Elizabeth.
A Pelican at Blandings, 1969

I gave him my Alpine hat. It made me feel like a father reluctantly throwing his child from the sledge to divert the attention of the pursuing wolf pack, as I believe happens all the time in Russia in the winter months.
Stiff Upper Lip, Jeeves, 1963

Many a man may look respectable, and yet be able to hide at will behind a spiral staircase.
'Success Story', *Nothing Serious*, 1950

Phoebe withdrew, sobbing softly and looking like a white rabbit that has had bad news from home.
Cocktail Time, 1958

His voice was virtually a coo, as if he had been a cushat dove in conference with another cushat dove.
Barmy in Wonderland, 1952

Her eyes and hair were a browny hazel. The general effect was of a seraph who ate lots of yeast.
'How's That, Umpire?', *Nothing Serious*, 1950

'Why are you looking like a bereaved tapeworm, Clarence?'
Pigs Have Wings, 1952

He looked like a Volga boatman who has just learned that Stalin has purged his employer.
'Excelsior', *Nothing Serious*, 1950

The years had been rough with Mortimer Bayliss, withering him till he now resembled something excavated from the tomb of one of the earlier Ptolemies. A testy fellow ... a human snapping turtle.
Something Fishy, 1957

He was uttering odd, strangled noises like a man with no roof to his mouth trying to recite 'Gunga Din'.
Jeeves and the Feudal Spirit, 1954

Old Mr Saxby looked like something stationed in a cornfield to discourage crows.
Cocktail Time, 1958

He gave me a long, reproachful look, similar in its essentials to that which a black beetle gives a cook when the latter is sprinkling insect powder on it.
Jeeves and the Feudal Spirit, 1954

Monica Simmons . . . a stalwart girl in a smock and breeches who looked like what in fact she was, one of the six daughters of a rural Vicar all of whom had played hockey for Roedean.
Pigs Have Wings, 1952

She exuded an aura of wealth. It showed itself in her rings, her hat, her stockings, her shoes, her platinum fur cape and the Jacques Fath sports costume that clung lovingly to her undulating figure. Here, you would have said to yourself, beholding her, was a woman who had got the stuff in sackfuls and probably suffered agonies from coupon-clipper's thumb, a woman at the mention of whose name the bloodsucking leeches of the Inland Revenue Department were accustomed to raise their filthy hats with a reverent intake of breath.
Ring for Jeeves, 1953

He heaved himself up in slow motion like a courtly hippopotamus rising from its bed of reeds on a riverbank.
Something Fishy, 1957

Barmy sat down heavily, as if his legs had been mown from under him. He felt as though his spine had been withdrawn from his body and a cheap spaghetti substitute inserted in its place.
Barmy in Wonderland, 1952

The stormy expression on Mr Anderson's face intensified. He might have been something Gutzon Borglum had carved on the side of a mountain. As so often when in Mervyn Potter's society, he was trying to think who it was he reminded himself of. Then he got it. Job. Job after he had lost his camels and acquired all those boils. Not that Job's sorrows could be compared with those of a man forced to associate with Mervyn Potter.
Barmy in Wonderland, 1952

He had a voice that sounded as though he ate spinach with sand in it.
Ring for Jeeves, 1953

'Somebody had inserted steak and onions in that dog – I sniffed his breath, and it was like opening the door of a Soho chophouse on a summer night – and the verdict of History will be that it was you.'
Pigs Have Wings, 1952

As I gave the cosh a suggestive waggle, Stilton's demeanour was that of an Assyrian who, having come down like a wolf on the fold, finds in residence not lambs but wild cats, than which, of course, nothing makes an Assyrian feel sillier.
Jeeves and the Feudal Spirit, 1954

Stilton Cheesewright is a man with a pink face and a head that looks as if it has been blown up with a bicycle pump.
Jeeves and the Feudal Spirit, 1954

I rather think, though I can't be sure, that at those words Stilton ground his teeth. Certainly there was a peculiar sound, as if a coffee mill had sprung into action.
Jeeves and the Feudal Spirit, 1954

He gave him a nasty look. It was a look that seemed to bring into the office an Edgar Allan Poe-like atmosphere of wailing winds and family curses.
Barmy in Wonderland, 1952

Lady Constance had winced at the sight of Lord Emsworth like a Greek goddess finding a caterpillar in her salad.
A Pelican at Blandings, 1969

He, too, seemed disinclined for chit-chat. We stood for some moments like a couple of Trappist monks who have run into each other by chance at the dog races.
Jeeves and the Feudal Spirit, 1954

My Aunt Dahlia proposing to sell *Milady's Boudoir*! It was like hearing that Rodgers had decided to sell Hammerstein!
Jeeves and the Feudal Spirit, 1954

A stern look came into Gally's face. A jellied eel seller who had seen it would have picked up his jellied eels and sought refuge in flight, like one who fears to be struck by lightning.
Pigs Have Wings, 1952

A musical voice . . . a voice like a good brand of Burgundy made audible.
Cocktail Time, 1958

Bobbie's outer crust was indeed of a nature to cause those beholding it to rock back on their heels with a startled whistle. But while equipped with eyes like twin stars, hair ruddier than the cherry, oomph, *espièglerie* and all the fixings, B. Wickham had all the disposition and general outlook on life of a ticking bomb.

Jeeves in the Offing, 1960

Spode reeled and uttered a cry like that of a cinnamon bear that has stubbed its toe on a passing rock.

Stiff Upper Lip, Jeeves, 1963

The Scottie-dog Bartholomew gave me an unpleasantly superior look, as if asking me if I were saved.

Stiff Upper Lip, Jeeves, 1963

'You suddenly bobbed up, Bertie, like a corpse rising to the surface of a sheet of water.'

Stiff Upper Lip, Jeeves, 1963

'Well,' she said, choking on the word like a Pekinese on a chump chop too large for its frail strength.

Jeeves and the Feudal Spirit, 1954

The basement of Bond's Bank smelled in equal proportions of mildew, old documents and mice.

Do Butlers Burgle Banks?, 1968

He sighed like a patronising escape of steam.

Company for Henry, 1967

The eyes behind Gussie's horn-rimmed spectacles gleamed with a brighter light, and a smile wreathed his lips. He looked like a fish that's just learned that its rich uncle in Australia has pegged out and left it a packet.

Stiff Upper Lip, Jeeves, 1963

Barribault's Hotel in Brook Street can make the wrong sort of client feel more like a piece of cheese – and a cheap yellow piece of cheese at that – than any other similar establishment in the world. The personnel of its staff are selected primarily for their ability to curl the upper lip and raise the eyebrows just that extra quarter of an inch which makes all the difference.

Full Moon, 1947

The Sergeant of Police who sat at his desk in the dingy little Paris police station was calm, stolid and ponderous, giving the impression of being constructed of some form of suet.
Frozen Assets, 1964

He had a pleasing and distinctive singing voice, not unlike that of a buzzard suffering from laryngitis.
Frozen Assets, 1964

There was a thought fluttering about the outskirts of his mind like a shortsighted dove seeking entry into a dovecot, and he could not pin it down.
Frozen Assets, 1964

Lord Emsworth had sunk back in his chair and was looking like the Good Old Man in old-fashioned melodrama when the villain has foreclosed the mortgage on the ancestral farm. There was not a great deal of flesh on his angular form, but what there was was creeping.
Galahad at Blandings, 1964

His face darkened. He looked like a halibut that's taken offence at a rude remark from another halibut.
Stiff Upper Lip, Jeeves, 1963

The Sergeant quivered a little like a suet pudding in a high wind.
Frozen Assets, 1964

Gally's bright eyes, one of them adorned with a black-rimmed monocle, seemed to be watching horses rounding into the straight, his neatly shod foot to be pawing in search of a brass rail.
Galahad at Blandings, 1965

It was with a distinctly fevered hand that Florence reached out for a dressing gown, and in her deportment, as she hopped from between the sheets, I noted a marked suggestion of a pea on a hot shovel.
Jeeves and the Feudal Spirit, 1954

It was not in Lord Emsworth's power to laugh bitterly, but he uttered a bleating sound which was as near as he could get to a bitter laugh.
Service with a Smile, 1962

One hand was under his head; the other, hanging down on the floor, looked like a strayed ham congealed into stone.

'The Debut of Battling Billson', *Ukridge*, 1924

She melted quite perceptibly. She did not cease to look like a basilisk, but she began to look like a basilisk who has had a good lunch.

The Girl on the Boat, 1922

He quivered like a smitten blanc-mange.

Sam the Sudden, 1925

He resembled a minor prophet who has been hit behind the ear with a stuffed eel-skin.

'Ukridge's Dog College', *Ukridge*, 1924

He oozed softly in like some soundless liquid.

Bill the Conqueror, 1924

Hash looked like one who has drained the four-ale of life and found a dead mouse at the bottom of the pewter.

Sam the Sudden, 1925

His manner had the offensive jauntiness of the man who has had a cold bath when he might just as easily have had a hot one.

The Girl on the Boat, 1922

Dolly gazed at him with the cold disdain of a princess confronted with a boll weevil.

Sam the Sudden, 1925

I sat among the elect on the platform at the Associated Mechanics' Hall, and there came up to me a mixed scent of dust, clothes, orange peel, chalk, wood, plaster, pomade, and Associated Mechanics . . . the whole forming a mixture which, I began to see, was likely to prove too rich for me. I changed my seat in order to bring myself next to a small but promising-looking door, through which it would be possible, if necessary, to withdraw without being noticed.

'The Long Arm of Looney Coote', *Ukridge*, 1924

It was a page torn from one of those illustrated weekly journals, faded and yellow, and over one corner a dark stain had spread itself, seeming to indicate that some occupant of the hut had at one time or another done a piece of careless carving. . . .

Hash surveyed the paper closely.

'That's mutton gravy,' he said, pointing at the stain and forming a professional man's swift diagnosis. 'Beef wouldn't be so dark.'

Sam the Sudden, 1925

John, they couldn't help noticing, looked like a murderer who had been doing physical jerks for years.

Money for Nothing, 1928

Her smile seemed to make the world on the instant a sweeter and better place. Policemen, when she flashed it on them after being told the way somewhere, became of a sudden gayer, happier policemen and sang as they directed the traffic. Beggars, receiving it as a supplement to a small donation, perked up like magic and started to bite the ears of the passers-by with an abandon which made all the difference. And when they saw that smile even babies in their perambulators stopped looking like peevish poached eggs and became almost human.

Sam the Sudden, 1925

A well-defined scent of grease, damp towels and old cabbages told her that the room through which she was creeping was the kitchen.

The Small Bachelor, 1927

He looked like a bookmaker who won billiard tournaments, and Kay gazed at him with repulsion.

Sam the Sudden, 1925

'I am Lord Tilbury,' said His Lordship, looking like a man unveiling a statue of himself.

Sam the Sudden, 1925

It was Pat's voice, sounding in the warm silence like moonlight made audible.

Money for Nothing, 1928

Chimp Twist was looking like a monkey that has bitten into a bad nut, and Soapy Molloy like an American Senator who has received an anonymous telegram saying 'All is discovered. Fly at once'. This sudden activity on the part of one whom they had regarded as under the influence of some of the best knock-out drops that ever came out of Chicago had had upon them an effect similar to that which would be experienced by a group of surgeons in an operating-theatre if the gentleman on the slab was to rise abruptly and begin to dance the Charleston.

Money for Nothing, 1928

I was feeling like a badly wrapped brown-paper parcel. I'm never at my best in the early morning.

'Extricating Young Gussie', *The Man with Two Left Feet*, 1917

. . . the head of a whacking great fish, lying on the carpet and staring up at me in a rather austere sort of way, as if it wanted an explanation and apology.

'Sir Roderick Comes to Lunch', *The Inimitable Jeeves*, 1923

'Seeing me strolling along the street,' said Ukridge, 'with the gloves, the cane, the spats, the shoes, and the old top-hat, you might wonder if I was a marquess or a duke, but you would be pretty sure I was one of the two.'

'A Bit of Luck for Mabel', *Eggs, Beans and Crumpets*, 1940

The orchestra started to play 'Poet and Peasant' and Sir Aylmer's face assumed the reverent, doughlike expression of attention so familiar in the rotundas of cure resorts.

'Romance at Droitgate Spa', *Eggs, Beans and Crumpets*, 1940

A sharp thrill permeated his frame and he sat up in his chair as if a new, firm backbone had been inserted in place of the couple of feet of spaghetti he had been getting along with up till now.

'Sonny Boy', *Eggs, Beans and Crumpets*, 1940

Lord Emsworth was a man who, in times of stress, always tended to resemble the Aged Parent in an old-fashioned melo-drama when informed that the villain intended to foreclose the mortgage. He wore now a disintegrated air, as if someone had

removed most of his interior organs. You see the same sort of thing in stuffed parrots when the sawdust has leaked out of them.
Uncle Fred in the Springtime, 1939

The Duke shot back in his chair, and his moustache, foaming upwards as if a gale had struck it, broke like a wave on the stern and rockbound coast of the Dunstable nose. A lesser moustache, under the impact of that quick, agonized expulsion of breath, would have worked loose at the roots.
Uncle Fred in the Springtime, 1939

A full-throated baying, a cross between a bloodhound on the trail and a Scotsman celebrating New Year's Eve.
Uncle Fred in the Springtime, 1939

A wintry contortion of his facial muscles which might have passed in a dim light for a smile.
Money in the Bank, 1946

He was a small man with the face of an untrustworthy monkey, the sort of monkey other monkeys would have shrunk from allowing to come within arm's reach of their nut ration.
Money in the Bank, 1946

Lord Uffenham had once more become remote and was looking like a recently unveiled statue.
Money in the Bank, 1946

There came into his eyes a sudden wild gleam of hope, such as might have come into the eyes of some wretched man on a scaffold, who, just as the executioner is spitting on his hands with a cheery 'Heave Ho!', observes a messenger galloping up on a foaming horse, waving a parchment.
Money in the Bank, 1946

Dolly Molloy was an attractive woman, but there were times when she could look more like a cobra about to strike than most cobras do.
Money in the Bank, 1946

Her voice was soft and tender, like that of a hen crooning over its egg.
Joy in the Morning, 1947

He fixed me with a cold and challenging eye, as if daring me to start something. I remember having seen the same defiant glitter behind the spectacles of a man I met in a country hotel once, just before he told me his name was Snodgrass.

Joy in the Morning, 1947

'Eeek!' cried Sally, squeaking like a mouse surprised while eating cheese.

Quick Service, 1940

A wooden expression had crept into his features, and his eyes had taken on the look of cautious reserve which you see in those of parrots, when offered half a banana by a stranger of whose bona fides they are not convinced.

Joy in the Morning, 1947

If that merger comes off, the milk of human kindness will slosh about in him like the rising tide, swamping all animosity.

Joy in the Morning, 1947

He was white and shaken, like a sidecar cocktail.

Quick Service, 1940

Like so many heavily moustached men, Mr Duff was unaware of the spiritual shock, akin to that experienced by Macbeth on witnessing the approach of the forest of Dunsinane, which the fungus had on nervous persons who saw it suddenly on its way towards them.

Quick Service, 1940

He was fingering his moustache nervously, like a foiled baronet in an old-time melodrama.

Money in the Bank, 1946

The eyes glaring, the moustache bristling and the *tout ensemble* presenting a strong resemblance to a short-tempered tiger of the jungle which has just seen its peasant shin up a tree.

Joy in the Morning, 1947

Lord Worplesdon has the manners of a bear disturbed when hibernating.

Joy in the Morning, 1947

Aunt Agatha is like an elephant – not so much to look at, for in appearance she resembles more a well-bred vulture – but because she never forgets.
Joy in the Morning, 1947

This young Hopwood is a blue-eyed little half-portion with, normally, an animated dial. The dial to which I refer was now contorted with anguish, as if she had just swallowed a bad oyster.
Joy in the Morning, 1947

A silence that you could have dug bits out of with a spoon.
'Jeeves Takes Charge', *Carry On, Jeeves*, 1925

He had just that expression of peeved surprise that one of those sheep's head fish in Florida has when you haul it over the side of the boat.
'Jeeves and the Chump Cyril', *My Man Jeeves*, 1919

Mrs Pringle's aspect was that of one who had had bad news round about the year 1900 and never really got over it.
'Without the Option', *Carry On, Jeeves*, 1925

A curious gulping noise not unlike a bulldog trying to swallow half a cutlet in a hurry so as to be ready for the other half.
'The Rummy Affair of Old Biffy', *Carry On, Jeeves*, 1925

Old Bittlesham quivered from head to foot like a pole-axed blanc-mange.
'Comrade Bingo', *The Inimitable Jeeves*, 1923

He started to get pink in the ears, and then in the nose, and then in the cheeks, till in about a quarter of a minute he looked pretty much like an explosion in a tomato cannery on a sunset evening.
'Jeeves and the Chump Cyril', *My Man Jeeves*, 1919

He gazed at me with misty eyes, as if he had taken a shade too much mustard with his last bite of ham.
'Bingo and the Little Woman', *The Inimitable Jeeves*, 1923

Lady Malvern fitted into my biggest arm-chair as if it had been built round her by someone who knew they were wearing arm-chairs tight around the hips that season.
'Jeeves and the Unbidden Guest', *Carry On, Jeeves*, 1925

He looked haggard and care-worn, like a Borgia who has suddenly remembered that he has forgotten to put cyanide in the consommé, and the dinner gong due any minute.

'Clustering Round Young Bingo', *Carry On, Jeeves*, 1925

. . . a look on his face as if someone had hit him behind the ear with a stuffed eel-skin.

'Bingo and the Little Woman', *The Inimitable Jeeves*, 1923

The swan made a hissing noise like a tyre bursting in a nest of cobras.

'Jeeves and the Impending Doom', *Very Good, Jeeves*, 1930

It isn't very often I find my own existence getting a flat tyre, but now the old nerves began to stick out of my body a foot long and curling at the ends.

'The Delayed Exit of Claude and Eustace', *The Inimitable Jeeves*, 1923

Bingo laughed in an unpleasant, hacking manner as if he were missing on one tonsil.

'Jeeves and the Old School Chum', *Very Good, Jeeves*, 1930

Biffy was jumping about like a lamb in the springtime – and, what is more, a feeble-minded lamb.

'The Rummy Affair of Old Biffy', *Carry On, Jeeves*, 1925

Something struck me a violent blow on the back hair, and I fell like some monarch of the forest beneath the axe of the woodman.

'Jeeves Makes an Omelette', *My Man Jeeves*, 1919

She executed a sort of leap or bound, not unlike a barefoot dancer who steps on a tin-tack half way through *The Vision of Salome*.

'Without the Option', *Carry On, Jeeves*, 1925

That poor old Bingo was knee-deep in the bisque was plain by his mere appearance – which was that of a cat which has just been struck by a half-brick and is expecting another shortly.

'Jeeves and the Impending Doom', *Very Good, Jeeves*, 1930

One of the first lessons life teaches us is that on these occasions of back-chat between the delicately-nurtured, a man should retire into the offing, roll up into a ball, and imitate the prudent

tactics of the opossum, which, when danger is in the air, pretends to be dead, frequently going to the length of hanging out crêpe and instructing its friends to stand round and say what a pity it all is.
  'Jeeves and the Old School Chum', *Very Good, Jeeves*, 1930

A man who could stay indoors cataloguing vases while his fiancée wandered in the moonlight with explorers deserved all that was coming to him.
  'A Mixed Threesome', *The Clicking of Cuthbert*, 1922

Honoria Glossop has a voice like a lion-tamer making some authoritative announcement to one of the troupe.
  'Without the Option', *Carry On, Jeeves*, 1925

He fell into the room rather in the manner of a dead body tumbling out of a cupboard in a mystery play and, colliding with Ambrose, clasped him in a close embrace, so that for an instant the thing resembled the meeting after long separation of a couple of Parisian boulevardiers of the old school.
  The Luck of the Bodkins, 1935

The memory comes back to you as you are dropping off to sleep, causing you to leap on the pillow like a gaffed salmon.
  The Code of the Woosters, 1938

Her eyes, which were large and dark and lustrous, like those of some inscrutable priestess of a strange old religion, focused themselves on him as she spoke, and seemed to go through him in much the same way as a couple of red-hot bullets would go through a pound of butter. He rocked back on his heels, feeling as if someone had stirred up his interior organs with an egg beater.
  'Feet of Clay', *Nothing Serious*, 1950

He saw Celia appear at the French windows and stand looking in: so he intensified the silent passion of his dancing, trying to convey the idea of being something South American, which ought to be chained up and muzzled in the interests of pure womanhood.
  'Tangled Hearts', *Nothing Serious*, 1950

'You'll be as cosy in here as a worm in a chestnut.'
  The Luck of the Bodkins, 1935

His eye, once so kindly, could have been grafted on to the head of a man-eating shark and no questions asked.

'The Juice of an Orange', *Blandings Castle*, 1935

His manner resembled that of a wolf on the steppes of Russia who, expecting a peasant, is fobbed off with a wafer biscuit.

'The Juice of an Orange', *Blandings Castle*, 1935

Reggie looked like a member of the Black Hand trying to plot assassinations while hampered by a painful gumboil. His manner was dark, furtive and agitated.

The Luck of the Bodkins, 1935

The RMS Atlantic was behaving more like a Russian dancer than a respectable ship. Ivor Llewellyn, prone in his bunk and holding on to the woodwork, was able to count no fewer than five occasions when the vessel lowered Nijinsky's record for leaping in the air and twiddling the feet before descending.

The Luck of the Bodkins, 1935

Mavis spoke in a voice that would have had an Eskimo slapping his ribs and calling for the steam heat.

'Fate', *Young Men in Spats*, 1936

Captain Bradbury drew him aside and gave him the sort of look he would have given a Pathan discovered pinching the old regiment's rifles out on the North-West Frontier.

'Trouble Down at Tudsleigh', *Young Men in Spats*, 1936

His standing with her was now approximately what King Herod's would have been at an Israelite Mothers Social Saturday Afternoon.

'Goodbye to All Cats', *Young Men in Spats*, 1936

A large, red-haired man in a sweater and corduroy trousers who looked as if he might be in some way connected with the jellied eel industry.

'The Masked Troubadour', *Lord Emsworth and Others*, 1937

A heavy-weight French mother with beetling brows who looked as if she had just come from doing a spot of knitting at the foot of the guillotine. Just to see those eyebrows, Freddie tells me, was to hear the heads dropping into the basket.

'Noblesse Oblige', *Young Men in Spats*, 1936

He shot up like a young Hindu fakir with a sensitive skin making acquaintance with his first bed of spikes.

The Luck of the Bodkins, 1935

This girl was not pretty. She was distinctly plain. Even ugly. She looked as if she might be a stenographer selected for some business magnate by his wife out of a number of competing applicants.

'Fate', *Young Men in Spats*, 1936

Elizabeth Bottsworth gave a sort of gurgling scream not unlike a coloratura soprano choking on a fish-bone.

'The Amazing Hat Mystery', *Young Men in Spats*, 1936

He tells me that he doubts if a chamois of the Alps, unless at the end of a most intensive spell of training, could have got down those stairs quicker than he did.

'Trouble Down at Tudsleigh', *Young Men in Spats*, 1936

Captain Bradbury's eyebrows had met across the top of his nose, his chin was sticking out from ten to fourteen inches, and he stood there flexing the muscles of his arms, making the while a low sound like the rumbling of an only partially extinct volcano. The impression Freddie received was that at any moment molten lava might issue from the man's mouth, and he wasn't absolutely sure that he liked the look of things.

'Trouble Down at Tudsleigh', *Young Men in Spats*, 1936

The goldfish made faces like Leslie Henson and withdrew.

Laughing Gas, 1936

Tiptoeing across the carpet with all the caution of a slack-wire artist who isn't any too sure he remembers the correct steps.

'Goodbye to All Cats', *Young Men in Spats*, 1936

The girl was like a chunk of ice cream with spikes all over it.

'Goodbye to All Cats', *Young Men in Spats*, 1936

I felt like that French general who brought up the reserves to the Battle of the Marne in taxi-cabs. Do you suppose he worried about the way the clock was going up? Of course not.

'The Come-Back of Battling Billson', *Lord Emsworth and Others*, 1937

Uttering a low, honking cry like that of some refined creature of the wild caught in a trap, Prudence Whittaker staggered back against the wall.

Summer Moonshine, 1938

Like so many substantial citizens of America, he had married young and kept on marrying, springing from blonde to blonde like the chamois of the Alps leaping from crag to crag.

Summer Moonshine, 1938

He was hungry. He continued to fold her in his arms, but it was with a growing feeling that he wished she had been a steak smothered in onions.

Summer Moonshine, 1938

'Peckish is not the word. I felt like a homeless tapeworm.'

Laughing Gas, 1936

Ann is one of those girls who always look as if they had just stepped out of a cold bath after doing their daily dozen.

Laughing Gas, 1936

He swallowed convulsively, like a Pekinese taking a pill.

The Code of the Woosters, 1938

He was loosely and comfortably dressed in a tweed suit which might have been built by Omar the Tent Maker.

Laughing Gas, 1936

A disciplinary light came into her fine eyes. She looked like a female lion-tamer about to assert her personality with one of the troupe.

'The Crime Wave at Blandings', *Lord Emsworth and Others*, 1937

He groaned slightly and winced, like Prometheus watching his vulture dropping in for lunch.

Big Money, 1931

He's as slippery as an eel that's been rubbed all over with axle-grease.

Money for Nothing, 1928

'Lady Constance looks on me as a sort of cross between a leper and a nosegay of deadly nightshade.'

Summer Lightning, 1929

Mr Gedge was leaning limply back in his seat blowing little air-bubbles. If the St Rocque undertaker could have beheld him now, he would have given him a very sharp look and instructed his assistants to get ready for a big rush of business.

Hot Water, 1932

He resembled a frog that had been looking on the dark side since it was a slip of a tadpole.

Aunts Aren't Gentlemen, 1974

He looked like a small-time gangster with a painful gumboil.

Aunts Aren't Gentlemen, 1974

Flossie was breathing like a bull-pup choking over a chicken bone.

'The Come-Back of Battling Billson', *Lord Emsworth and Others*, 1937

She spoke in a low voice, like beer trickling out of a jug.

The Code of the Woosters, 1938

He paused to mop a moist brow. He had something of the emotions of a rabbit that has just eluded a more than usually quick-tempered boa-constrictor.

Hot Water, 1932

A tough-looking man in one of those tight suits which somehow seem to suggest dubious morals.

Hot Water, 1932

The bottle had the subtly grim look of champagne which has been bought at a public house.

If I Were You, 1931

His eyes were like the eyes of a fish not in the best of health.

Big Money, 1931

Even in repose, her manner was forceful. Of her past life before their marriage, except that she was the widow of a multi-millionaire oil man named Brewster who had left her all his multi-millions, Mr Gedge knew nothing. He sometimes thought she might have been a lion-tamer.

Hot Water, 1932

He sat down at the table. His face, which in repose resembled a slab of granite with suspicious eyes, was softened now by a genial smile. He had not actually parked his gun in the cloak-room, but he had the air of a man who has done so.

Hot Water, 1932

He vanished like an eel into mud.

Hot Water, 1932

He was hopping about like a carefree cat on hot bricks.

The Code of the Woosters, 1938

She heaved a sigh which seemed to come straight up from the cami-knickers.

The Code of the Woosters, 1938

His hostess's resemblance to a leopardess was now so vivid that the room seemed to have bars and an odd smell. Only the presence of a man in a peaked cap and a few bones lying about the floor were needed to complete the Regent's Park atmosphere.

Summer Moonshine, 1938

There had always been something distinctive and individual about Gussie's voice, reminding the hearer partly of an escape of gas from a gas pipe and partly of a sheep calling to its young in the lambing season.

The Code of the Woosters, 1938

Roderick Spode . . . a chap who, even in repose, would have made an all-in wrestler pause and pick his words.

The Code of the Woosters, 1938

Like all antique shops it was dingy outside and dark and smelly within. I don't know why it is, but the proprietors of these establishments always seem to be cooking some sort of a stew in the back room.

The Code of the Woosters, 1938

Roderick Spode was a big chap with a small moustache and the sort of eye that can open an oyster at sixty paces.
The Code of the Woosters, 1938

He looked like a Dictator on the point of starting a purge.
The Code of the Woosters, 1938

Gulping a bit from time to time, like a fish that has been landed out of a pond on a bent pin and isn't at all sure it is equal to the pressure of events.
The Code of the Woosters, 1938

While Monty Bodkin was not actually spatted at the moment, there did undoubtedly hang about him a sort of spat aura.
Heavy Weather, 1933

'I'm scared', she said. 'It's this place. It's so big and old. It makes me feel like a puppy that's got into a cathedral.'
Heavy Weather, 1933

'This,' he said, 'is like being in heaven without going to all the bother and expense of dying.'
Hot Water, 1932

Lord Tilbury rose from his chair and began to pace the room. Always Napoleonic of aspect, being short and square and stumpy and about twenty-five pounds overweight, he looked now like Napoleon taking his morning walk at St Helena.
Heavy Weather, 1933

It was one of those vases which a Zulu chieftain would have been perfectly satisfied to make shift with while his knobkerrie was being cleaned at the club-maker's.
Hot Water, 1932

I retired to an arm-chair and put my feet up, sipping the mixture with carefree enjoyment, rather like Caesar having one in his tent the day he overcame the Nervii.
Right Ho, Jeeves, 1934

He made a noise like a pig swallowing half a cabbage.
Thank You, Jeeves, 1934

'Oh, I'm not complaining,' said Chuffy, looking rather like Saint Sebastian on receipt of about the fifteenth arrow.
Thank You, Jeeves, 1934

I began to feel like some wild thing caught in a snare.
Right Ho, Jeeves, 1934

His portion of turbot was a rather obscene-looking mixture of bones and eyeballs and black mackintosh.
Heavy Weather, 1933

She sank bewildered on the cushions with all the sensations of one who, after being cut by the County, walks into a brick wall.
Heavy Weather, 1933

'You must surge round him like glue.'
Heavy Weather, 1933

He looked like a cat in an adage.
Right Ho, Jeeves, 1934

There was nothing of the lion leaping from its den about the way I now left the bedroom, but rather a bit more the suggestion of a fairly diffident snail poking its head out of its shell during a thunderstorm.
Thank You, Jeeves, 1934

The heavy breathing that came through the window could only be that of a parsimonious man occupied in writing a cheque for a thousand pounds. It is a type of breathing which it is impossible to mistake, though in some respects it closely resembles the sound of a strong man's death agony.
Heavy Weather, 1933

He was a man who was musing on the coming Social Revolution. He said nothing, merely looking at me as if he were measuring me for my lamp-post.
Thank You, Jeeves, 1934

In my experience there are two kinds of elderly American. One, the stout and horn-rimmed, is matiness itself. He greets you as if you were a favourite son, starts agitating the cocktail shaker before you know where you are, slips a couple into you with a merry laugh, claps you on the back, tells you a dialect story about two Irishmen named Pat and Mike, and, in a word, makes life one grand, sweet song. The other, which runs a good deal to the cold, grey stare and the square jaw, seems to view the English cousins with concern. He is not Elfin. He broods. He says little. He sucks in his breath in a pained way. And every now and again you catch his eye, and it is like colliding with a raw oyster.

Thank You, Jeeves, 1934

Uncle Tom always looked a bit like a pterodactyl with a secret sorrow.

Right Ho, Jeeves, 1934

As for Gussie Fink-Nottle, many an experienced undertaker would have been deceived by his appearance and started embalming him on sight.

Right Ho, Jeeves, 1934

'You must go there, and flock round her like a poultice.'

Right Ho, Jeeves, 1934

And, giving me the sort of weak smile Roman gladiators used to give the Emperor before entering the arena, Gussie trickled off.

Right Ho, Jeeves, 1934

He had been looking like a dead fish. He now looked like a deader fish, one of last year's, cast up on some lonely beach and left there at the mercy of the wind and tides.

Right Ho, Jeeves, 1934

When at this juncture he stepped back and folded his arms with a bitter sneer, it was as if he had jabbed her in the eye with a burnt stick.

Thank You, Jeeves, 1934

Conditions being as they were at Brinkley Court – I mean to say, the place being loaded down above the Plimsoll mark with aching hearts and standing room only as regards tortured souls – I hadn't expected the evening meal to be particularly effervescent. Nor was it. Silent. Sombre. The whole thing more than a bit like Christmas dinner on Devil's Island.

Right Ho, Jeeves, 1934

An expression like that of a young Hindu fakir who, having settled himself on his first bed of spikes, is beginning to wish that he had chosen one of the easier religions.
Heavy Weather, 1933

She passed from the room looking like something out of an Edgar Allan Poe story.
Right Ho, Jeeves, 1934

She unshipped a sigh that sounded like the wind going out of a rubber duck.
Right Ho, Jeeves, 1934

If you can visualise a bulldog which has just been kicked in the ribs and had its dinner sneaked by the cat, you will have Hildebrand Glossop as he now stood before me.
Right Ho, Jeeves, 1934

Her face now was pale and drawn, like that of a hockey centre-forward at a girls' school who, in addition to getting a fruity one on the shin, has just been penalised for 'sticks'.
Right Ho, Jeeves, 1934

I wedged myself in among the standees at the back, leaning up against a chap who, from the aroma, might have been a corn-chandler or something of that order.
Right Ho, Jeeves, 1934

Jeeves doesn't have to open doors. He's like one of those birds in India who bung their astral bodies about – the chaps, I mean, who, having gone into thin air in Bombay, reassemble the parts and appear two minutes later in Calcutta.
Right Ho, Jeeves, 1934

An eerie silence seemed to envelop the room like a linseed poultice. I happened to be biting on a slice of apple in my fruit salad at the moment, and it sounded as if Carnera had jumped off the top of the Eiffel Tower on to a cucumber frame.
Right Ho, Jeeves, 1934

I was stunned. I began to understand how a general must feel when he has ordered a regiment to charge and has been told that it isn't in the mood.
Right Ho, Jeeves, 1934

Lord Hoddesdon felt a little like a tiger which has hoped for a cut off the joint and has been handed a cheese straw.
Big Money, 1931

'Yes,' said Millicent, rather in the tone of voice which Schopenhauer would have used when announcing the discovery of a caterpillar in his salad.
Summer Lightning, 1929

Pilbeam slipped through the door of his bedroom, banged it and was gone. Many an eel has disappeared into the mud with less smoothness and celerity.
Summer Lightning, 1929

He was lean and athletic-looking. He had the appearance of a welter-weight boxer who takes a cold bath every morning and sings in it.
Big Money, 1931

A sharp cry escaped Sir Gregory. His face had turned a deep magenta. In these affluent days of his middle age, he always looked rather like a Regency buck who has done himself well for years among the flesh-pots. He now resembled a Regency buck who, in addition to being on the verge of apoplexy, has been stung in the leg by a hornet.
Summer Lightning, 1929

She looked like something that might have occurred to Ibsen in one of his less frivolous moments.
Summer Lightning, 1929

He was the sort of man who would have tried to cheer Napoleon up by talking about the Winter Sports at Moscow.
Summer Lightning, 1929

He eyed the sunbeam as if it wanted to borrow money from him.
Big Money, 1931

Ricky's heart seemed to leap straight up into the air twiddling its feet, like a Russian dancer. He had sometimes wondered how fellows in the electric chair must feel when the authorities turn on the juice. Now he knew.
Uncle Fred in the Springtime, 1939

His resemblance to a fox with a pack of hounds and a bevy of the best people on its trail, had become pronounced.
Uncle Fred in the Springtime, 1939

Bingo swayed like a jelly in a high wind.
'The Editor Regrets', *Eggs, Beans and Crumpets*, 1940

From the young man there had proceeded a bubbling grunt like that of some strong swimmer in his agony.
Uncle Fred in the Springtime, 1939

A sudden, sinister calm fell upon the Duke, causing his manner to resemble that of a volcano which is holding itself in by sheer will-power.
Uncle Fred in the Springtime, 1939

She shoots her eyes at you without turning her head, as if she were a basilisk with a stiff neck.
'A Bit of Luck for Mabel', *Eggs, Beans and Crumpets*, 1940

He stood gaping at her, his heart bounding about inside him like an adagio dancer with nettle-rash.
'All's Well with Bingo', *Eggs, Beans and Crumpets*, 1940

She looked like a woman of good family who kept cats.
'Big Business', *A Few Quick Ones*, 1959

Myra had been walking with bowed head, as if pacing behind the coffin of a dear and valued friend.
Service with a Smile, 1962

At Barribault's Hotel the carpets are of so thick a nap that midgets would get lost in them and have to be rescued by dogs.
Ice in the Bedroom, 1961

A happy vision rose before Chimp's eyes, of Mrs Thomas G. Molloy sinking for the third time in some lake or mere and himself, with a sneer on his lips, throwing her an anvil.
Ice in the Bedroom, 1961

His IQ was somewhat lower than that of a backward clam – a clam, let us say, which has been dropped on its head when a baby.
Barmy in Wonderland, 1952

The Paris bistro was full of taxi-drivers and men who looked as if they were taking a coffee break after a spell of work in the sewers.
Frozen Assets, 1964

Lady Hermione Wedge was short and dumpy and looked like a cook – in her softer moods a cook well satisfied with her latest soufflé; when stirred to anger a cook about to give notice; but always a cook of strong character.
Galahad at Blandings, 1964

He reminded me of a genial old eighteenth-century squire in the coloured supplement of a Christmas number presiding over a dinner to the tenantry.
'Success Story', *Nothing Serious*, 1950

Wilfred Allsop was sitting up, his face pale, his eyes glassy, his hair disordered. He looked like the poet Shelley after a big night out with Lord Byron.
Galahad at Blandings, 1965

His resemblance to a corpse that had been in the water several days was still pronounced, but it had become a cheerier corpse, one that had begun to look on the bright side.
Galahad at Blandings, 1965

He looked haggard and haunted. He reminded Lancelot of a rabbit with a good deal on its mind.
'Cats Will be Cats', *Mulliner Nights*, 1933

A hearty voice that seemed to boom through the garden like a costermonger calling attention to his Brussels-sprouts.
Joy in the Morning, 1947

It was a dark night, without a moon or any rot of that sort. Stars, yes. Moon, no. A lynx might have seen me, but only a lynx, and it would have had to be a pretty sharpsighted lynx, at that.
Joy in the Morning, 1947

The raw excitements and jungle conditions of Steeple Bumpleigh must have come upon him as a totally new experience,
causing him to wonder what had hit him – like a man, stooping
to pluck a nosegay of wild flowers on a railway line, unexpectedly struck in the small of the back by the Cornish Express.
Joy in the Morning, 1947

He clicked his tongue. To me it sounded like a mass meeting of
Spanish dancers playing the castanets.
Joy in the Morning, 1947

She quivered gently, as if in the early stages of palsy, and her
face, as far as I could gather, was pale and set, like the white of a
hard-boiled egg.
Joy in the Morning, 1947

I uttered a stricken cry, like a cat to whom the suggestion has
been made that she part with her new-born kitten.
Joy in the Morning, 1947

She came leaping towards me, like Lady Macbeth coming to get
first-hand news from the guest-room.
Joy in the Morning, 1947

Uncle Percy was waving a cigar menacingly, like the angel
expelling Adam from the Garden of Eden.
Joy in the Morning, 1947

He felt dazed and bewildered, as if he had been swimming in a
sea of glue and had swallowed a good deal of it.
'The Story of Webster', *Mulliner Nights*, 1933

Dame Daphne blinked as if she had been struck on the mazzard
with a wet dish-cloth.
The Mating Season, 1949

Lord Emsworth had not supposed that in these degenerate days
a family like this existed. The sister copped Angus McAllister
on the shin with stones, the brother bit Constance in the leg. . . .

It was like listening to some grand old saga of the exploits of heroes and demigods.
    'Lord Emsworth and the Girl Friend', *Blandings Castle and Elsewhere*, 1935

It's a rummy feeling when you've got yourself all braced for the fray and suddenly discover that the fray hasn't turned up. Rather like treading on the last stair when it isn't there.
    Joy in the Morning, 1947

He had a rather morose expression on his face, like an elephant that has had its bun taken from it.
    The Mating Season, 1949

Rugged sea captains, accustomed to facing gales in the Western Ocean without a tremor, quivered like blancmanges when hauled up before Lord Worplesdon in his office and asked why the devil they had – or had not – ported the helm or spliced the main-brace during their latest voyage in his service. In disposition akin to a more than ordinarily short-tempered snapping turtle, he resembled in appearance a malevolent Aubrey Smith, and usually, when one encountered him, gave the impression of being just about to foam at the mouth.
    Joy in the Morning, 1947

The general's eye was piercing him through and through, and every moment he felt more like a sheep that has had the misfortune to encounter a potted meat manufacturer.
    'The Bishop's Move', *Meet Mr Mulliner*, 1927

The drowsy stillness of the summer afternoon was shattered by what sounded to his strained senses like G. K. Chesterton falling on a sheet of tin.
    'The Story of Cedric', *Mr Mulliner Speaking*, 1929

A shrill, bat-like, middle-aged bachelor squeak.
    'The Story of Cedric', *Mr Mulliner Speaking*, 1929

A small tapping sound that might have been the first tentative efforts of a very young woodpecker just starting out in business for itself.
    'Something Squishy', *Mr Mulliner Speaking*, 1929

Covering his face with his hands, he sank on the bench, feeling like a sandbagged leper.

'Unpleasantness at Bludleigh Court', *Mr Mulliner Speaking*, 1929

I collapsed into a chair as if the lower limbs had been mown off with a scythe.

Joy in the Morning, 1947

He could set the full force of his iron personality playing over the fellow like a hose.

'The Voice from the Past', *Mulliner's Nights*, 1933

Boko uttered a sharp, yapping sound, like a displeased hyena.

Joy in the Morning, 1947

It was as if a stick of dynamite had been touched off beneath me. The hair rose in a solid mass and every nerve in the body stood straight up, curling at the ends.

Joy in the Morning, 1947

He gave me one of those looks of his, and it chilled my insides like a quart of ice cream.

Joy in the Morning, 1947

The train was disgorging passengers at every door. It was the sort of mob-scene that would have made David W. Griffith scream with delight; and it looked, George says, like Guest Night at the Royal Automobile Club.

'The Truth about George', *Meet Mr Mulliner*, 1927

A beastly laugh, like glue pouring out of a jug.

'The Bishop's Move', *Meet Mr Mulliner*, 1927

George stammered. He produced a sort of sizzling sound like a cockroach calling to its young.

'The Truth about George', *Meet Mr Mulliner*, 1927

Uncle Percy had crumpled like a wet sock. He sank into a chair, and clutched the marmalade jar, as if for support. His eyes popped out of his head, and waved about on their stalks. He appeared to have turned into a pillar of salt. If it hadn't been that the ginger whiskers were quivering gently, you would have said that life had ceased to animate the rigid limbs.

Joy in the Morning, 1947

Angus McAllister, the head gardener, was a man with a Clydeside accent and a face like a dissipated potato.

'Lord Emsworth and the Girl Friend', *Blandings Castle and Elsewhere*, 1935

The medicine had a slightly pungent flavour, rather like old boot-soles beaten up in sherry.

'Mulliner's Buck-U-Uppo', *Meet Mr Mulliner*, 1927

The staff consisted of an aged cook who, as she bent over her cauldrons, looked like something out of a travelling company of *Macbeth*, touring the smaller towns of the North, and Murgatroyd the butler, a huge, sinister man, with a cast in one eye and an evil light in the other.

'A Slice of Life', *Meet Mr Mulliner*, 1927

The last time she had seen Sacheverell he had been the sort of man who made a shrinking violet look like a Chicago gangster. And here he was now, staring her in the eye and shooting his head off for all the world as if he were Mussolini informing the Italian Civil Service of a twelve per cent cut in their weekly salary.

'The Voice from the Past', *Mulliner Nights*, 1933

Most people, eyeing him, would have been reminded of a corpse that had been several days in the water.

'The Nodder', *Blandings Castle and Elsewhere*, 1935

With a gesture such as Job might have made on discovering a new boil, he crossed to the window and stood looking moodily out.

'The Story of Webster', *Mulliner Nights*, 1933

Mr Potter uttered a low, curious sound, like a cat with a fish-bone in its throat.

'Mr Potter Takes a Rest Cure', *Blandings Castle and Elsewhere*, 1935

A sigh like the whistling of the wind through the cracks of a broken heart escaped Lady Wickham.

'Mr Potter Takes a Rest Cure', *Blandings Castle and Elsewhere*, 1935

When she spoke it was with the mildness of a cushat dove addressing another cushat dove from which it was trying to borrow money.

Jeeves in the Offing, 1960

They withdrew, laughing heartily, like a couple of intoxicated ambassadors who have delivered their credentials to a reigning monarch and are off to get a few more quick ones before the bar closes.

Barmy in Wonderland, 1952

Smedley sniffed at his glass of yoghurt with a shrinking distaste, and gave it as his opinion that it smelled like a motorman's glove.

The Old Reliable, 1951

In moments of excitement she had that extraordinary habit of squeaking like a basketful of puppies.

Spring Fever, 1948

Filled with the coward rage that dares to burn but does not dare to blaze, Lord Emsworth coughed a cough that was undisguisedly a bronchial white flag.

'Lord Emsworth and the Girl Friend', *Blandings Castle and Elsewhere*, 1935

It was as though something blunt and heavy had hit her on the head at the exact moment when she was slipping on a banana skin.

'Unpleasantness at Bludleigh Court', *Mr Mulliner Speaking*, 1929

His monocle shot forth flame.

Full Moon, 1947

A fatuous smile of self-satisfaction illuminated the young man's face, giving him the appearance of a beaming sheep.

'The Custody of the Pumpkin', *Blandings Castle and Elsewhere*, 1935

His hat was on the side of his head and he bore his cigar like a banner.

Uncle Dynamite, 1948

Nature, doubtless with the best motives, had given Stanwood, together with a heart of gold, a face like that of an amiable hippopotamus. And everybody knows that unless you are particularly fond of hippopotami, a single cursory glance at them is enough. Many blasé explorers do not even take that.

Spring Fever, 1948

On Pongo's face a close observer would have noted at the moment an austere, wary look such as might have appeared on St Anthony's just before the temptations began.

Uncle Dynamite, 1948

Myrtle Prosser was a woman of considerable but extremely severe beauty. She did not resemble her father, who looked like a cassowary, but suggested rather one of those engravings of the mistresses of Bourbon kings which make one feel that the monarchs who selected them must have been men of iron, impervious to fear, or else shortsighted.

Ice in the Bedroom, 1961

Honoria Glossop was one of those large, strenuous, dynamic girls with the physique of a middle-weight catch-as-catch-can wrestler and a laugh resembling the sound of the Scotch Express going under a bridge. The effect she had on me was to make me slide into a cellar and lie low till they blew the All Clear.

'Jeeves and the Greasy Bird', *Plum Pie*, 1966

A frown appeared on Mr Bunting's face. Normally it resembled that of an amiable vulture. He looked now like a vulture dissatisfied with its breakfast corpse.

'Life with Freddie', *Plum Pie*, 1966

He felt like a General who, having devised a plan of campaign calling for the whole line to advance, goes to the camp and sees his troops loafing about there with cigarettes and mouthorgans, the last thing in their minds a forward movement.

Company for Henry, 1967

Jane was a small, fair-haired girl who looked like a well-dressed wood nymph.

Company for Henry, 1967

He had presented, as so many members of the Pelican Club did, the appearance of a man with a severe hangover who had slept in his clothes and had not had time to shave.

A Pelican at Blandings, 1969

Joe Bender was looking terrible. A man, to use an old-fashioned phrase, of some twenty-eight summers, he gave the impression of having experienced at least that number of very hard winters.

A Pelican at Blandings, 1969

Lady Constance started irritably, like the Statue of Liberty stung by a mosquito which had wandered over from the Jersey marshes.

A Pelican at Blandings, 1969

Lord Emsworth had dreamt that he had gone to the sty, eagerly anticipating the usual feast for the eye, and there before him had stood a lean, streamlined Empress, her ribs clearly defined and her whole aspect that of a pig which had been in hard training for weeks, the sort of pig that climbs Matterhorns and wins the annual Stock Exchange walk from London to Brighton.

A Pelican at Blandings, 1969

It made her feel as if her nerve centres had been scrubbed with sandpaper.

A Pelican at Blandings, 1969

Ginger hadn't the meagre chance of a toupee in a high wind.

Much Obliged, Jeeves, 1971

He had the look of a man who was coming down with at least three of the exotic ailments which get written up in special numbers of *The Lancet*. Monty had seen dead fish on fishmongers' slabs with more sparkle and *joie de vivre*.

Pearls, Girls and Monty Bodkin, 1972

The doctor felt my pulse and tapped me all over like a whiskered woodpecker.

Aunts Aren't Gentlemen, 1974

I was somewhat piqued at being accused of bellowing by a woman whose lightest whisper was like someone calling the cattle home across the sands of Dee.

Much Obliged, Jeeves, 1971

He was cold and hard, like a picnic egg.
Much Obliged, Jeeves, 1971

How true is the old saying, attributed to Pliny the Elder, that a man who lets himself get above himself is simply asking for it, for it is just when things seem to be running as smooth as treacle out of a jug that he finds Fate waiting for him round the corner with the stuffed eelskin.
The Girl in Blue, 1970

As Soapy admiringly put it, Dolly's fingers just flickered, making the whole shoplifting operation seem as simple as taking sweets from a sleeping child.
Pearls, Girls and Monty Bodkin, 1972

It seared his soul as if he had backed into a red hot radiator in the bathroom.
Pearls, Girls and Monty Bodkin, 1972

A tear was stealing down Sally's cheek, and crying women always made him feel as if he were wearing winter woollies during a heat wave.
Bachelors Anonymous, 1973

Mrs McCorkadale was what I would call a grim woman. She had a beaky nose, tight thin lips, and her eye could have been used for splitting logs in the teak forests of Borneo.
Much Obliged, Jeeves, 1971

A stout man with a face rather like that of a vulture which had been doing itself too well on the corpses.
'The Castaways', *Blandings Castle and Elsewhere*, 1935

He was a tough, hard-bitten retired Colonial Governor of the type which comes back to England to spend the evenings of its days barking at club waiters.
'The Code of the Mulliners', *Young Men in Spats*, 1936

He withdrew, walking on the tips of his toes and conveying in his manner the suggestion that if he had had a hat and that hat had contained roses, he would have started strewing them from it.

The Mating Season, 1949

Lady Hermione stopped hammering on the table with a teaspoon. It was like a lightning strike in a boiler factory.

Full Moon, 1947

Horror made her words come out in a dry whisper, preceded by an odd, crackling sound which it would have taken a very sharp-eared medical man to distinguish from a death-rattle.

Full Moon, 1947

His soul was seething in rebellion like a cistern struck by a thunderbolt.

Uncle Dynamite, 1948

He was built on large lines, and seemed to fill the room to overflowing. In physique he was not unlike what Primo Carnera would have been if Carnera hadn't stunted his growth by smoking cigarettes when a boy.

'Open House', *Mulliner Nights*, 1933

A ladder, even the medium-sized one which he had found, is not a light burden, but he made nothing of it. He carried it like a clouded cane. There were moments when he came near to flicking it.

Full Moon, 1947

The Empress resembled a captive balloon with ears and tail, and was as nearly circular as a pig can be without bursting.

'Pig-Hoo-o-o-o-ey!', *Blandings Castle and Elsewhere*, 1935

The spreading fields of wheat took on the appearance of velvet rubbed the wrong way as the light breeze played over them.

Spring Fever, 1948

There came to his ears a sudden, loud, gurgling noise rather like that which might have proceeded from a pig suffocating in a vat of glue. It was the sound of someone snoring.

'The Story of Cedric', *Mr Mulliner Speaking*, 1929

A slow, pleasant voice, like clotted cream made audible.
Full Moon, 1947

Prudence made a tired gesture, like a Christian martyr who has got a bit fed up with lions.
Full Moon, 1947

Lady Constance uttered a sound which resembled that caused by placing a wet thumb on a hot stove lid.
Pigs Have Wings, 1952

Bingo uttered a quick howl like that of a Labrador timber wolf which has stubbed its toe on a jagged rock.
'The Shadow Passes', *Nothing Serious*, 1950

Esmond Haddock looked like a combination of a poet and an all-in wrestler. It would not have surprised you to learn that he was the author of sonnet sequences of a fruity and emotional nature which had made him the toast of Bloomsbury, for his air was that of a man who could rhyme 'love' and 'dove' as well as the next chap. Nor would you have been astonished if informed that he had recently felled an ox with a single blow. You would simply have felt what an ass the ox must have been to get into an argument with a fellow with a chest like that.
The Mating Season, 1949

On his face was the sort of look which might have been worn by a survivor of the last days of Pompeii.
'Feet of Clay', *Nothing Serious*, 1950

He shuddered, and in addition to shuddering, uttered a sharp quack of anguish such as might have proceeded from some duck which, sauntering in a reverie beside the duck-pond, has inadvertently stubbed its toe on a broken soda-water bottle.
Cocktail Time, 1958

A vocal delivery rather reminiscent of a bad-tempered toastmaster.
Uncle Dynamite, 1948

A cold hand seemed to clutch at my heart. I felt like a Gadarene swine that had come within a toucher of doing a nose-dive over the precipice.
The Mating Season, 1949

'I'm just a worm in a gilded cage.'
The Old Reliable, 1951

Even on his good days he looked a little like something thrown off by Epstein in a particularly sombre mood, and this was not one of his good days.
Barmy in Wonderland, 1952

Her face was shining like the seat of a bus-driver's trousers.
Jeeves and the Feudal Spirit, 1954

He eyed her apprehensively like some rat of the underworld cornered by G-men.
Pigs Have Wings, 1952

He was gnashing his teeth and filling the air with a sound similar to that produced by an inexperienced Spanish dancer learning to play the castanets.
'Scratch Man', *A Few Quick Ones*, 1959

The fishy glitter in his eye became intensified. He looked like a halibut which has just been asked by another halibut to lend it a couple of quid till next Wednesday.
'The Word in Season', *A Few Quick Ones*, 1959

Lord Tilbury had an ingrained dislike for parting with large sums of money. There was, and always had been, something about signing his name to substantial cheques that gave him a sort of faint feeling.
Service with a Smile, 1962

'I have got L. G. Trotter's number all right. His attitude towards Ma Trotter is that of an exceptionally diffident worm towards a sinewy Plymouth Rock or Orpington. A word from her and he curls up into a ball.'
Jeeves and the Feudal Spirit, 1954

There was a wardrobe and he dived into it like a seal going after a chunk of halibut.
'Success Story', *Nothing Serious*, 1950

The next instant there had cut piercingly into the summer stillness a sudden sharp wail that seemed to tell of a human being in mortal distress. It was the voice of Lord Emsworth raised in song.

'Company for Gertrude', *Blandings Castle and Elsewhere*, 1935

He perceived Lord Emsworth at his side, drooping like a tired lily. Except when he had something to prop himself against, there was always a suggestion of the drooping floweret about the master of Blandings Castle. He seemed to work on a hinge somewhere in the small of his back, and people searching for something nice to say about him sometimes described him as having a scholarly stoop.

Service with a Smile, 1962

'Ever seen driven snow?'
    'I know the sort of snow you mean.'
    'Well, that's what I'm as pure as.'
    Ice in the Bedroom, 1961

The Duke of Dunstable's standing among his neighbours in Wiltshire was roughly that of a shark at a bathing resort – something, that is to say, to be avoided on all occasions as nimbly as possible.

Service with a Smile, 1962

He gave the book a tentative prod with the tip of his fingers, like a puppy pawing at a tortoise.

Spring Fever, 1948

HERE
AND
THERE

'How absurdly simple these things are when you have someone with elephantiasis of the brain, like myself, directing the operations.'
Uncle Dynamite, 1948

She was the sort of girl, so familiar a feature of the English countryside, who goes about in brogue shoes and tweeds and meddles vigorously in the lives of the villagers, sprucing up their manners and morals till you wonder that something in the nature of a popular uprising does not take place.
Spring Fever, 1948

Bingo was standing on the steps, looking bereaved to the gills.
'Bramley is So Bracing', *Nothing Serious*, 1950

The indefinable air of not intending to part with fivers.
'Success Story', *Nothing Serious*, 1950

'Cummere!' said Mrs Carlisle, and there entered from the bedroom a tall, slender, almost excessively gentlemanly man in a flowered dressing-gown, who might have been the son of some noble house or a Latin-American professional dancer.
Cocktail Time, 1958

Otis Painter was walking to and fro with his mouth open and his knees clashing like cymbals, for he had the misfortune to suffer from adenoids and to be knock-kneed.
Uncle Dynamite, 1948

Muriel gnashed her teeth in a quiet undertone.
'The Voice from the Past', *Mulliner Nights*, 1933

Adela is what is technically known as a tough baby. Her bite spells death.
Spring Fever, 1948

Bill was a splendidly virile young man, and if you had had a mad bull you wished dealt with, you could have placed it in no better hands.

Full Moon, 1947

'It was as though a bevy of expectant wolves had overtaken a sleigh and found no Russian peasant aboard, than which I can imagine nothing more sickening. For the wolves, of course.'

Uncle Dynamite, 1948

Some workmen were busy tearing up the paving with pneumatic drills, but the whirring of Freddie's brain made the sound almost inaudible.

'Company for Gertrude', *Blandings Castle and Elsewhere*, 1935

Sir Aylmer Bostock's collection of African curios which he had collected during his years of honourable exile was probably the most hideous, futile and valueless that ever an ex-Governor had brought home with him, and many of its items seemed to take Pongo into a different and dreadful world.

Uncle Dynamite, 1948

These cases of mistaken identity are very common. There was a man at the Pelican Club who was the living image of one of the Cabinet Ministers, which made it very awkward for the latter, as the Pelican chap was always getting thrown out of restaurants, frequently wearing a girl's hat.

Galahad at Blandings, 1964

'I haven't felt so relieved since the afternoon in West Africa when a rhinoceros, charging at me with flashing eyes, suddenly sprained an ankle and had to call the whole thing off.'

'A Good Cigar is a Smoke', *Plum Pie*, 1966

As a dancer I out-Fred the nimblest Astaire.

Joy in the Morning, 1947

Unseen, in the background, Fate was quietly slipping the lead into the boxing-glove.

'Jeeves and the Old School Chum', *Very Good, Jeeves*, 1930

Ambrose had gone to bed in a condition of sandbagged pessimism.

The Luck of the Bodkins, 1935

He would have felt kindlier towards him if he had bathed more recently and had smelled less strongly of unsweetened gin.
'The Masked Troubadour', *Lord Emsworth and Others*, 1937

Captain Bradbury's right eyebrow had now become so closely entangled with his left that there seemed no hope of ever extricating it without the aid of powerful machinery.
'Trouble Down at Tudsleigh', *Young Men in Spats*, 1936

'You don't like her?'
'I regard her as the sand in Civilisation's spinach.'
Summer Moonshine, 1938

Billson was standing there with his customary air of thinking hard about absolutely nothing, and Flossie made for him like a peroxided leopardess.
'The Come-Back of Battling Billson', *Lord Emsworth and Others*, 1937

Like all patrons of coffee-stalls, they were talking about the Royal Family.
Sam the Sudden, 1925

Major Plank's tan was so deep that it was impossible to say whether or not he paled beneath it, but he shuddered violently and in his eyes was the look that comes into the eyes of men who peer into frightful abysses.
Uncle Dynamite, 1948

Only the fact that I should have upset the breakfast tray prevented me from turning my face to the wall. When Esmond Haddock had spoken of the times that try men's souls, he hadn't a notion of what the times that try men's souls can really be if they spit on their hands and get right down to it. I levered a forkful of kipper and passed it absently over the larynx, endeavouring to adjust the faculties to a set-up which even the most intrepid would have had to admit was a honey.
The Mating Season, 1949

Freddie had mooned about with an air of crushed gloom that would have caused comment in Siberia.
Something Fresh, 1915

Those women were drawing their skirts away as I passed. They shivered when I spoke to them. From time to time I would catch them looking at me in a way that would have wounded a smash-and-grab man.
The Mating Season, 1949

'You can never trust these old Indian Army men, Corky. Heroes, all of them, and it gets them greatly disliked.'
'Ukridge and the Home from Home', *Lord Emsworth and Others*, 1937

Like all Baronets, he had table-thumping blood in him.
Summer Moonshine, 1938

So, though he would much have preferred to go to Whipsnade and try to take a mutton chop away from a tiger, Freddie had a couple of quick ones, ate a clove and set off.
'The Masked Troubadour', *Lord Emsworth and Others*, 1937

It was plainly his intention to resume the attack from another and less well-guarded quarter. This, I believe, is a common manoeuvre on the North-West Frontier. You get your Afghan shading his eyes and looking out over the *maidan*, and then you sneak up the *pahar* behind him and catch him bending.
'Trouble Down at Tudsleigh', *Young Men in Spats*, 1936

The barmaid's ears began to work loose at the roots as she pricked them up.
'Tried in the Furnace', *Young Men in Spats*, 1936

'Have you ever, Corky, during a friendly political discussion in a pub, been punched squarely on the nose?'
'Ukridge and the Home from Home', *Lord Emsworth and Others*, 1937

You can't swat a man who is thanking you for saving his life, not if your own is ruled by the *noblesse oblige* code of the Widgeons.
'The Masked Troubadour', *Lord Emsworth and Others*, 1937

The practice of ships' doctors of always grabbing the prettiest girl on board and carrying her off to play quoits or deck tennis is

one of the most disturbing phenomena of ocean travel, and it is one that has caused many a young man to chew the lower lip and scowl with drawn brows. Monty found his resentment against this frivolous pill-slinger growing more and more intense as the minutes went by. There were a thousand things the fellow ought to have been doing – looking at people's tongues, extracting people's appendices, bottling the mixture as before or even just sitting in his cabin with his text-books, brushing up his medical knowledge. Instead of which, there he stood, laughing all over his fat face, bunging quoits at a wooden peg with Lottie Blossom.
The Luck of the Bodkins, 1935

'The natives seemed fairly friendly, so I decided to stay the night.'
I made a mental note never to seem fairly friendly to an explorer. If you do, he always decides to stay the night.
'A Mixed Threesome', *The Clicking of Cuthbert*, 1922

'Ha, ha, ha, ha, ha,' he replied with scarcely veiled derision.
'Up From the Depths', *Nothing Serious*, 1950

The football referee was either filled with the spirit of Live and Let Live or else had got his whistle choked up with mud.
'The Ordeal of Young Tuppy', *Very Good, Jeeves*, 1930

I ate cheese gravely.
'The Letter of the Law', *Lord Emsworth and Others*, 1937

'He won't have a leg to stand on.'
'It seems that he'll have one leg to stand on while he kicks me with the other.'
'Jeeves and the Chump Cyril', *My Man Jeeves*, 1919

Whether anyone was ever at his ease in the society of this old Gawd-help-us, I cannot say, but I definitely was not. The spine, and I do not attempt to conceal the fact, had become soluble in the last degree.
Joy in the Morning, 1947

He ground a tooth or two. It was plain that he was in a dangerous mood.
Joy in the Morning, 1947

Mrs Cork had once had a native bearer who, when given his orders for the day, had said 'Why?' You can recognise him easily, if you happen to be in his village, by the dazed, stunned look which still lingers on his face and the way he has of jumping, if anyone speaks to him suddenly.

Money in the Bank, 1946

He danced like something dark and slithery from the Argentine.

'Feet of Clay', *Nothing Serious*, 1950

Fate, if it slips us a bit of good with one hand, is pretty sure to give us the sleeve across the windpipe with the other.

Uncle Dynamite, 1948

My heart, ceasing to stand still, gave a leap and tried to get out through my front teeth.

The Mating Season, 1949

A licentious clubman operating on all twelve cylinders.

Uncle Dynamite, 1948

Her eyes were dark with pain, and she was eating buttered toast in a crushed sort of way.

Full Moon, 1947

She found him seated at the table, playing chess with himself. From the contented expression on his face, he appeared to be winning.

Money in the Bank, 1946

A cold, aloof, non-bonhomous old blister. . . .

Money in the Bank, 1946

'I have a memory like a steel trap, but it doesn't always work as it should.'

Money in the Bank, 1946

Too many cooks, in baking rock cakes, get misled by the word 'rock', and it was into this category that Ma Balsam fell.
Money in the Bank, 1946

He gave one of those short, quick, roopy coughs by means of which solicitors announce that a conference is concluded.
Money in the Bank, 1946

There came into her eyes, softening their steely glitter for a moment, that strange light which is seen in the eyes of confirmed public speakers who are asked to say a few words.
'A Bit of Luck for Mabel', *Eggs, Beans and Crumpets*, 1940

Pongo staggered to a chair. He sat down heavily. And some rough indication of his frame of mind may be gathered from the fact that he forgot to pull the knees of his trousers up.
Uncle Fred in the Springtime, 1939

His voice had become pink and he was twiddling his fingers and shuffling his feet.
'Romance at Droitgate Spa', *Eggs, Beans and Crumpets*, 1940

When pleasing inspirations floated into Lord Ickenham's mind, the prudent man made for the nearest bombproof shelter.
Uncle Fred in the Springtime, 1939

'The Duke is tough. He nails his collar to the back of his neck to save buying studs.'
Uncle Fred in the Springtime, 1939

In 'Mustard' Pott he discovered that he had come up against one of the Untouchables. Beginning by quoting from Polonius's speech to Laertes, which a surprising number of people whom you would not have suspected of familiarity with the writings of Shakespeare seem to know, Mr Pott had gone on to say that lending money always made him feel as if he were rubbing velvet the wrong way, and that in any case he would not lend it to Pongo, because he valued his friendship too highly. The surest method of creating a rift between two pals, explained Mr Pott, was for one pal to place the other pal under a financial obligation.
Uncle Fred in the Springtime, 1939

Preux to the last drop.
   Uncle Fred in the Springtime, 1939

'Mustard' Pott walked slowly, with bowed head, for he was counting ten-pound notes.
   Uncle Fred in the Springtime, 1939

Long experience has taught me that innocence pays no dividends. Pure as the driven snow though he may be, or even purer, it is the man on the spot who gets the brickbats.
   Joy in the Morning, 1947

It's the old problem, of course – the one that makes life so tough for murderers – what to do with the body.
   The Code of the Woosters, 1938

Pongo bared his teeth in a bitter smile.
   Uncle Fred in the Springtime, 1939

In another half-jiffy I was about to slip a stick of dynamite under the old buster which would teach him that we are not put into the world for pleasure alone. When a magistrate has taken five quid off you for what, properly looked at, was a mere boyish peccadillo which would have been amply punished by a waggle of the forefinger and a brief 'Tut, tut', it is always agreeable to make him jump like a pea on a hot shovel.
   The Code of the Woosters, 1938

'Nuts to you, R. P. Crumbles!' he cried, with a strange dignity.
   'Excelsior', *Nothing Serious*, 1950

'Smedley is a poor sheep who can't say boo to a goose.'
   'Well, name three sheep who can.'
      The Old Reliable, 1951

Stanwood, a doughty performer on the football field during his college career, was a mass of muscle and bone, and it was Mr Cobbold's opinion that the bone extended to his head. Excellent at blocking a punt or giving a playmate the quick sleeve across the windpipe, but not bright.
   Spring Fever, 1948

He was either a man of about a hundred and fifty who was rather young for his years or a man of about a hundred and ten who had been aged by trouble.

'Lord Emsworth Acts for the Best', *Blandings Castle and Elsewhere*, 1935

Major Plank relapsed into a sandbagged silence.

Uncle Dynamite, 1948

'You see before you Frederick Altamont Cornwallis, fifth Earl of Ickenham, and one of the hottest earls that ever donned a coronet.'

Uncle Dynamite, 1948

'In less than no time I shall be bounding about the place trying to evade supertax.'

'Buried Treasure', *Lord Emsworth and Others*, 1937

The rule by which he had always lived was that the best would have to do till something better came along.

Do Butlers Burgle Banks?, 1968

'Lord Emsworth dislikes competent secretaries. They bother him and get on his nerves. They keep him from evading his responsibilities.'

Galahad at Blandings, 1964

'It's just zeal, Clarence. You get it in the young. She's a trier.'

'I find her trying,' Lord Emsworth retorted, one of the most brilliant things he had ever said. It was so good that he repeated it, and Gally gave another sympathetic nod.

Galahad at Blandings, 1964

Compared to French red tape that of Great Britain and America is only pinkish. Where, in the matter of rules and regulations, London and New York merely scratch the surface, these Gauls plumb the depths. It is estimated that a French minor official, with his heart really in his work, can turn more hairs grey and have more clients tearing those hairs than any six of his opposite numbers on the pay rolls of other nations.

Frozen Assets, 1964

'He'll probably be an ambassador some day.'

'Thus making a third world war inevitable.'

Frozen Assets, 1964

Crazy as a bed bug.
Frozen Assets, 1964

. . . mad as a wet hen.
Frozen Assets, 1964

'I always predicted that he would be successful. I never actually saw him talking into three telephones at the same time, for he had not yet reached those heights, but it was obvious that the day would come when he would be able to do it without difficulty.'
Service with a Smile, 1962

Rugby football is more or less a sealed book to me. But even I could see that Stinker was good. The lissomness with which he moved hither and thither was most impressive, as was his homicidal ardour when doing what I believe is called tackling. Like the Canadian Mounted Police he always got his man and when he did so the air was vibrant with the excited cries of morticians in the audience making bids for the body.
Stiff Upper Lip, Jeeves, 1963

'I don't quite know,' said Freddie Widgeon, 'how you set out growing coffee, but one soon gets to pick these things up. I am convinced that, given a spade and a watering can and shown the way to the bushes, it will not be long before I electrify the industry, raising a sensational bean. Kenya Ho! is the slogan.'
Ice in the Bedroom, 1961

'I have always had the ability to touch the human heart strings,' said Gally complacently. 'Why, in my early days, when I was at the top of my form, I have sometimes made bookies cry.'
Galahad at Blandings, 1964

It was only inadvertently that the Duke of Dunstable ever allowed anyone to finish a sentence.
A Pelican at Blandings, 1969

The hearts of Porky Jupp and Plug Bosher were broken into hash. When they wiped their gravy up with bread, they did it dully, and there was a listlessness in the way they chivvied bits of roly-poly pudding about the plate with their fingers which told its own story.
'Oofy, Freddie and the Beef Trust', *A Few Quick Ones*, 1959

'I don't know whether I am standing on my head or my heels.'
'Sift the evidence. At which end of you is the ceiling?'
Cocktail Time, 1958

He was in much the same position as a General who, with his strategic plans all polished and ready to be carried out, finds that his army has gone off somewhere, leaving no address.
Cocktail Time, 1958

It was fortunate for Cosmo that he had already consumed his roly-poly pudding, for, if he had not, it would have turned to ashes in his mouth.
Cocktail Time, 1958

'Prison's all right for a visit, I always say, but I wouldn't live there if you gave me the place.'
Cocktail Time, 1958

As fine a young fellow as he had ever met and one who – a rarity in Russell Clutterbuck's experience – though handicapped by being a Frenchman, did not louse things up by talking French all the time.
French Leave, 1956

A private investigator who learns that he is saving a client a hundred thousand dollars is a private investigator who puts his prices up.
Something Fishy, 1957

Eating gooseberries in an overwrought sort of way.
Jeeves and the Feudal Spirit, 1954

A grateful multi-millionaire was what he had been scouring the country for for years.
French Leave, 1956

'I don't know, Corky, if you have ever done the fine, dignified thing, refusing to accept money because it was tainted and there wasn't enough of it,' said Ukridge.
'Success Story', *Nothing Serious*, 1950

He was a strong, ambidextrous talker, whom it was hard to interrupt.
'Salvatore's Wrong Moment', *Indiscretions of Archie*, 1921

Reggie was a rather melancholy young man who suffered from elephantiasis of the bank-roll.

'Reggie Comes to Life', *Indiscretions of Archie*, 1921

'Great pal of mine, Squiffy. We went through Eton, Oxford and the Bankruptcy Court together.'

'Squiffy's Disturbed Night', *Indiscretions of Archie*, 1921

Boil the whole question of old age down, and what it amounts to is that a man is young as long as he can dance without getting lumbago, and, if he cannot dance, he is never young at all.

'The Man with Two Left Feet', *The Man with Two Left Feet*, 1917

Beale's passion for the truth had made him unpopular in three regiments.

Love Among the Chickens, 1906

When it comes to money – why, George is the fellow that made the dollar bill famous. He and Rockefeller have got all there is, except a little bit they have let Andy Carnegie have for car-fare.

A Damsel in Distress, 1919

He wore the unmistakable look of a man about to be present at a row between women, and only a wet cat in a strange back yard bears itself with less jauntiness than a man faced with such a prospect.

Piccadilly Jim, 1918

Among his friends at the Green-Room Club it was unanimously held that Walter Jelliffe's cigars brought him within the scope of the law forbidding the carrying of concealed weapons.

'Bill the Bloodhound', *The Man with Two Left Feet*, 1917

'Hang it!' said Bill to himself in the cab, 'I'll go to America!' The exact words probably which Columbus had used, talking the thing over with his wife.

Uneasy Money, 1917

He had selected a corner of the Club reading room because silence was compulsory there, thus rendering it possible for two men to hear each other speak.

Uneasy Money, 1917

Larsen's Exercises are the last word in exercises. They bring into play every sinew of the body. They promote a brisk circulation. They enable you, if you persevere, to fell oxen, if desired, with a single blow.
Something Fresh, 1915

The usual drawback to success is that it annoys one's friends so.
'The Man Upstairs', *The Man Upstairs*, 1914

In a speech which began as an argument and ended as pure cheek, she utterly routed the constable.
'Something to Worry About', *The Man Upstairs*, 1914

Inherited wealth, of course, does not make a young man nobler or more admirable, but the young man does not always know this.
A Gentleman of Leisure, 1910

I am told by one who knows that hens cannot raise their eyebrows, not having any; but I am prepared to swear that at this moment this hen raised hers. I will go further. She sniffed.
Love Among the Chickens, 1906

Lord Emsworth had had a bright idea and it had taken his breath away. This always happened when he had bright ideas. He had had one in the Spring of 1921 and another in the Summer of 1933, and those had taken his breath away, too.
'Birth of a Salesman', *Nothing Serious*, 1950

He started 'The Rosary' again, and stubbed his finger on a semi-quaver.
'Fixing It for Freddie', *Carry On, Jeeves*, 1925

A youth and middle age spent on the London Stock Exchange had left Lester Carmody singularly broad-minded. He had to a remarkable degree that precious charity which allows a man to look indulgently on any financial project, however fishy, provided he can see a bit in it for himself.
Money for Nothing, 1928

If the Cohen Bros., of Covent Garden, have a fault, it is that they sometimes allow their clients to select clothes that are a shade too prismatic for anyone who is not at the same time purchasing a banjo and a straw hat with a crimson ribbon.
Sam the Sudden, 1925

Sergeant-Major Flannery's moustache was long and blonde and bushy, and it shot heavenwards into two glorious needle-point ends, a shining zareba of hair quite beyond the scope of any mere civilian. Non-army men may grow moustaches and wax them and brood over them and be fond and proud of them, but to obtain a waxed moustache in the deepest and holiest sense of the words you have to be a Sergeant-Major.

Money for Nothing, 1928

'I don't say I've ever sold Central Park or Brooklyn Bridge to anybody, but if I can't get rid of a parcel of home-made oil stock to a guy that lives in the country, I'm losing my grip and ought to retire.'

Money for Nothing, 1928

'That's the way to get on in the world – by grabbing your opportunities. Why, what's Big Ben but a wrist watch that saw its chance and made good?'

The Small Bachelor, 1927

He snuggled into a laurel bush and waited.

Bill the Conqueror, 1924

'I'm not a safe-smasher. I'm a delicately nurtured girl that never used an oxy-acetylene blowpipe in her life.'

The Small Bachelor, 1927

And Ukridge left, without borrowing even a cigar, a sure sign that his resilient spirit was crushed beyond recuperation.

'Ukridge Sees Her Through', *Ukridge*, 1924

A spasm of Napoleonic strategy seized Sam. He dropped silently to the floor and concealed himself under the desk. Napoleon was always doing that sort of thing.

The Girl on the Boat, 1922

They train bank clerks to stifle emotion, so that they will be able to refuse overdrafts when they become managers.

'Ukridge's Accident Syndicate', *Ukridge*, 1924

A brief inspection of Blair Eggleston on the previous evening had satisfied him that the latter was just about the size he liked people to be on whom he planned committing assault and battery, and he was full of fight.

Hot Water, 1932

Gentlemanly to the last, he raised his hat again and stepped haughtily into the bushes.
Hot Water, 1932

Glowing with the fervour which comes to men about to chastise libertines smaller than themselves, he burst from the bushes.
Hot Water, 1932

'If England wants a happy, well fed aristocracy, she mustn't have wars. She can't have it both ways.'
Big Money, 1931

'The horse kicked me. Three times in the same place. Blimey, if I sat down now, I'd leave a hoof-print.'
If I Were You, 1931

The two lawyers then left, chatting amiably about double bur-gage, heirs taken in socage, and other subjects which always crop up when lawyers get together.
Big Money, 1931

'I can't stand Paris. I hate the place. Full of people talking French, which is a thing I bar. It always seems to me so affected.'
Big Money, 1931

Egbert and Percy, the two swans, had turned in for the night. Each was floating with its head tucked under the left wing; and if there is a spectacle more devoid of dramatic interest than a swan with its head tucked under its wing, it is two swans in that position.
Big Money, 1931

There had been a decade in Gregory Parsloe's life, that danger-ous decade of the twenties, when he had accumulated a past so substantial that a less able man would have been compelled to spread it over a far longer period.
Summer Lightning, 1929

A gloomy cave or dug-out that led to the heating apparatus of the hothouses. . . . The place was a sort of Sargasso Sea into which had drifted all the flotsam and jetsam of the kitchen garden which it adjoined. There were broken pots in great profusion. There was a heap of withered flowers, a punctured watering can, a rake with large gaps in its front teeth, some potatoes unfit for human consumption and half a dead blackbird.

Summer Lightning, 1929

'Very good,' I said coldly. 'In that case, tinkerty-tonk.' And I meant it to sting.

Right Ho, Jeeves, 1934

'Have you no delicacy, no proper feeling?'
    'No.'
    'Oh? Well, right-ho, of course, but I think you ought to have.'
    Right Ho, Jeeves, 1934

'These are mere straws, Jeeves. Do not let us chop them.'
    Right Ho, Jeeves, 1934

Gussie, a glutton for punishment, stared at himself in the mirror.

Right Ho, Jeeves, 1934

He was a man who, after a lifetime of doing down the widow and orphan, had begun to feel the strain a bit. His conversation was odd and he had a tendency to walk on his hands.

Thank You, Jeeves, 1934

I felt uplifted to no little extent, and you might say I was simply so much pure spirit, without any material side to me whatever.

Thank You, Jeeves, 1934

'You're great friends?'
    'Bosom is the *mot juste*.'
    Thank You, Jeeves, 1934

My earnest hope is that the entire remainder of my existence will be one round of unruffled monotony.

Thank You, Jeeves, 1934

I was behind the desk, crouching on the carpet and trying to breathe solely through the pores.
Thank You, Jeeves, 1934

There is enough sadness in life without having fellows like Gussie Fink-Nottle going about in sea-boots as a Pirate Chief.
Right Ho, Jeeves, 1934

For the last two days, since the departure of that young fellow Carmody, Lord Emsworth had had no secretary; and a man can't be expected to attend to his correspondence without a secretary. His conscience, accordingly, was clear.
Heavy Weather, 1933

'Sneak back to your room and barricade the door. That is the manly policy.'
Right Ho, Jeeves, 1934

It was only the fact of his teeth having snapped together with his tongue in between that had prevented his heart leaping out of his mouth.
Hot Water, 1932

If not actually disgruntled, he was far from being gruntled.
The Code of the Woosters, 1938

If the Drones Club tie has a fault, it is a little on the loud side and should not be sprung suddenly on nervous people and invalids.
Aunts Aren't Gentlemen, 1974

'Stiffy' Halliday was one of the many for whom the Pelican Club's pace had proved too rapid. He had signed his last IOU in his early forties, and it was a matter of surprise to his circle of inmates that he had managed to continue functioning till then.
A Pelican at Blandings, 1969

I remained where I was, merely hitching my ears up another couple of notches in order not to miss the rest of the dialogue.
Much Obliged, Jeeves, 1971

'. . . a psychiatrist.'
   'A what?'
   'One of those fellows who ask you questions about your childhood and gradually dig up the reason why you go about shouting "Fire!" in crowded theatres. They find it's because

somebody took away your allday sucker when you were six.'

'. . . I thought they were called head-shrinkers.'

'That, I believe, is the medical term.'
A Pelican at Blandings, 1969

Ferdie the Fly had the invaluable gift of being able to climb up the side of any house you placed before him, using only toes, fingers and personal magnetism.
Do Butlers Burgle Banks?, 1968

'When he suggested five pounds a week with board and lodging thrown in,' said Ukridge, 'it was all I could do to keep from jumping at it, for my financial position was not good. But I managed to sneer loftily, and in the end I got him up to ten.'
'Ukridge Starts a Bank Account', *Plum Pie*, 1966

She was a conscientious secretary. It was this defect in her character that so exasperated Lord Emsworth. His ideal secretary would have been one who breakfasted in bed, dozed in an armchair through the morning, played golf in the afternoon and took the rest of the day off.
Galahad at Blandings, 1964

The Captain was on the bridge, pretty sure that he knew the way to New York but, just to be on the safe side, murmuring to himself 'Turn right at Cherbourg and then straight on.'
'Life with Freddie', *Plum Pie*, 1966

All his life he had had a strong distaste for being hit on the nose, and it was on the nose, something told him, that Biff would hit him first.
Frozen Assets, 1964

He would have treated with the utmost respect any young man so obviously capable of a sweet left hook followed by a snappy right to the button.
Service with a Smile, 1962

Oofy Prosser was sitting in a corner, pale and haggard beneath his pimples.
'The Shadow Passes', *Nothing Serious*, 1950

'I was up at Oxford with the man. A blighter, if there ever was one. He was President of the Union and all sorts of frightful things.'
'Mr Potter Takes a Rest Cure', *Blandings Castle and Elsewhere*, 1935

Bill had been reduced to a state of almost soluble discomfort.
Full Moon, 1947

Lord Emsworth had one of those minds capable of accommodating but one thought at a time – if that.
'The Custody of the Pumpkin', *Blandings Castle and Elsewhere*, 1935

A ray of sunshine, which had been advancing jauntily along the carpet, caught sight of his face and slunk out, abashed.
'Lord Emsworth Acts for the Best', *Blandings Castle and Elsewhere*, 1935

Joe Beamish had at one time been a fairly prosperous burglar. Seeing the light after about sixteen prison sentences, he had given up his life work and now raised vegetables and sang in the choir.
'Anselm Gets his Chance', *Eggs, Beans and Crumpets*, 1940

Why is there unrest in India? Because its inhabitants eat only an occasional handful of rice. The day when Mahatma Gandhi sits down to a good juicy steak and follows it up with roly-poly pudding and a spot of Stilton you will see the end of all this nonsense of Civil Disobedience.
'The Juice of an Orange', *Blandings Castle and Elsewhere*, 1935

Joe Beamish was knitting a sock in the tiny living room which smelled in equal proportions of mice, ex-burglars and shag tobacco.
'Anselm Gets his Chance', *Eggs, Beans and Crumpets*, 1940

Neatly dressed in blue serge and shaved to the core.
'The Story of Webster', *Mulliner Nights*, 1933

. . . the fanatic gleam which comes into the eyes of all fat men who are describing their system of diet.
'A Slice of Life', *Meet Mr Mulliner*, 1927

One prefers, of course, on all occasions to be stainless and above reproach, but, failing that, the next best thing is unquestionably to have got rid of the body.
Joy in the Morning, 1947

'When I bop them, they stay bopped till nightfall.'
Jeeves in the Offing, 1960

'Unquestionably,' said Sir Roderick Glossop, 'his metabolism is unduly susceptible to stresses resulting from the interaction of external excitations.' Bobbie patted him on the shoulder in a maternal sort of way, a thing I wouldn't have cared to do myself, and told him he had said a mouthful.
Jeeves in the Offing, 1960

'I want to wear bank notes next my skin winter and summer, ten-pound ones in the chilly months, changing to fivers as the weather gets warmer.'
Ice in the Bedroom, 1961

The Empress . . . that bulbous mass of lard and snuffle.
Service with a Smile, 1962

It wrenched the heart-strings to have to ladle out bad tidings to the eager young prune, but the painful task could not be avoided.
Joy in the Morning, 1947

He strode off into the darkness, full to the brim with dudgeon.
Joy in the Morning, 1947

'Boy Scouts never sleep.'
'Of course they do. In droves.'
Joy in the Morning, 1947

His reputation is that of a man who, if there are beans to be spilled, will spill them with a firm and steady hand. He has never kept a secret and never will. His mother was frightened by a BBC announcer.
Spring Fever, 1948

If there is a chance that suavity will ease a situation, the Woosters always give it a buzz.
Joy in the Morning, 1947

Frederick had been under the impression that Nanny Wilks was fully six feet tall, with the shoulders of a weight-lifter and eyes that glittered cruelly beneath beetling brows. What he saw now was a little old woman with a wrinkled face, who looked as if a puff of wind would blow her away.

'Portrait of a Disciplinarian', *Meet Mr Mulliner*, 1927

It is never difficult to distinguish between a Scotsman with a grievance and a ray of sunshine.

'The Custody of the Pumpkin', *Blandings Castle and Elsewhere*, 1935

The awful thing that had come upon me had practically turned me into a pillar of salt. I doubt if the moth, or whatever it was that was doing Swedish exercises in and around my left ear, had the remotest notion that it had parked itself on the person of a once vivacious young clubman. A tree, it probably thought, or possibly even the living rock.

Joy in the Morning, 1947

He picked up the leg of mutton and began to gnaw it with an affected daintiness.

'The Ordeal of Osbert Mulliner', *Mr Mulliner Speaking*, 1929

I shot out an aghastish puff of smoke.

Joy in the Morning, 1947

Only the necessity of keeping both hands on the handlebars prevented him patting himself on the back.

Spring Fever, 1948

He was in the acute stage of that malady which, for want of a better name, scientists call the heeby-jeebies.

Spring Fever, 1948

It's an iron-clad contract, and if she attempts to slide out of it, she'll get bitten to death by wild lawyers.

Spring Fever, 1948

He put the two-seater into first. It seemed to him, as he did so, that the gears were a bit noisy. But it was only Tipton Plimsoll grinding his teeth.

Full Moon, 1947

Valerie's lips were trembling, and the bit of chicken which she had been raising to her mouth fell from her listless fork.
'The Shadow Passes', *Nothing Serious*, 1950

'Glug!' said Lord Emsworth – which, as any philologist will tell you, is the sound which peers of the realm make when stricken to the soul while drinking coffee.
'Lord Emsworth and the Girl Friend', *Blandings Castle and Elsewhere*, 1935

The partiality of drowning men for straws is proverbial; but, as a class, they are broad-minded and will clutch at punt-poles with equal readiness.
'Mr Potter Takes a Rest Cure', *Blandings Castle and Elsewhere*, 1935

He drank coffee with the air of a man who regretted it was not hemlock.
'Lord Emsworth and the Girl Friend', *Blandings Castle and Elsewhere*, 1935

A politician's trained verbosity.
'Mr Potter Takes a Rest Cure', *Blandings Castle and Elsewhere*, 1935

He felt he needed air. A similar sensation had often come to sensitive native chiefs at the conclusion of an interview with Sir Aylmer Bostock on the subject of unpaid hut taxes.
Uncle Dynamite, 1948

'Well, I think I'll mooch along and have a cup of tea,' he said, and mooched, as foreshadowed.
Uncle Dynamite, 1948

There is only one real cure for grey hair. It was invented by a Frenchman. He called it the guillotine.
The Old Reliable, 1951

I don't know if you have ever seen a fellow curvet, but war-horses used to do it rather freely in the old days, and Esmond Haddock was doing it now. His booted feet spurned the carpet in a sort of rhythmic dance.
The Mating Season, 1949

'When the porterhouse steak comes along, wade into it with your head down and your elbows out at right angles.'
  'Success Story', *Nothing Serious*, 1950

He waved a concerned cigar.
  Jeeves and the Feudal Spirit, 1954

He talks French with both hands.
  Ring for Jeeves, 1953

'As the car drove in at the gate, we struck a bumpy patch, and I could hear the milk of human kindness sloshing about inside him.'
  Pigs Have Wings, 1952

He groaned civilly in response to my greeting.
  'Joy Bells for Walter', *A Few Quick Ones*, 1959

'Don't be afraid. The only character who could pop in would be the Brinkley Court ghost. If it does, give it a cold look and walk through it. That'll teach it to come butting in when it isn't wanted, ha, ha.'
  Jeeves in the Offing, 1960

The temperature dropped noticeably. A snail that was passing at the time huddled back into its shell with the feeling that there was quite a nip in the air these mornings, and would have slapped its ribs, if it had had any.
  Ice in the Bedroom, 1961

Bill sat down and·put his head between his hands. A hollow groan escaped him, and he liked the sound of it and gave another.
  Ring for Jeeves, 1953

'Oofy Prosser declined to be my banker, as did my banker.'
  Ice in the Bedroom, 1961

Her hat was a frightful object, but it was still in the ring.
  'Feet of Clay', *Nothing Serious*, 1950

Foggy between the ears.
  Jeeves in the Offing, 1960